Benny Hill
KING LEER

THIS IS A CARLTON BOOK

Copyright © Essential Books Limited 2000

This edition published by Carlton Books Limited 2000
20 Mortimer Street
London
W1N 7RD

A CIP catalogue for this book is available from the British Library.

ISBN 1 8422 2214 7

Pictures supplied by: Mander & Mitchison pages 55, 58, 64
Pearson Television pages 6, 11, 30, 31, 34, 42, 43, 47, 50, 51, 67, 82, 87, 90, 95, 98, 102/3, 106, 111, 114, 115, 127
Pictorial Press pages 15, 19, 23, 24, 38, 68/9, 71, 76/7, 94
Rex Features pages 10, 13, 83, 122
SIPA-Press page 118
The author and publishers have made every reasonable effort to contact all copyright holders. Any errors that may have occurred are inadvertent and anyone who for any reason has not been contacted is invited to write to the publishers so that a full acknowledgement may be made in subsequent editions of this work.

Printed and bound in U.A.E.

Benny Hill
KING LEER

JEREMY NOVICK

CARLTON
BOOKS

By the same author

Morecambe & Wise: You Can't See the Join
Tommy Cooper: Just Like That
Wham Bam Thank You Glam

For LouLou

And . . . as ever to Gilly, Elly, Maxwell C. Wolf and Lexa – perfectly formed and more than a boy could reasonably ask for

And to my mum. Benny loved his and I love mine. So there.

Acknowledgements

I'd like to thank everyone who helped me, from Mary at the *Express* (the finest of all researchers), to Sacha and Eva who kept those pesky kids at bay, to my father who held my hand and provided unseen support, to my mother who laughed and complained that I wasn't going out "dressed like that". To Mal and John for shamelessly delegating the grief to Paul, to Margaret Forwood who said "another book about Benny!", to Dennis Kirkland for being willing if not able (but he's one of the good men so he gets a mention), to the producer, the lighting cameraman, the 2nd assistant director . . . I can't tell you how much all this means.

Bibliography

Benny Hill, Master Of Mirth – Robert Ross (Batsford)
Benny: The True Story – Dennis Kirkland and Hilary Bonner (Smith Gryphon)
The Illustrated Benny Hill – Gary Morecambe (Elm Tree Books)
The Real Benny Hill – Margaret Forwood (Robson Books)
Saucy Boy – Leonard Hill (Robson Books)

Contents

Author's Note

I CAN'T remember the year. I remember sitting around the family television one evening and we were watching *The Benny Hill Show* and there was a sketch on where Benny was dressed up as this Chinese man – all black slicked-back hair and slitty eyes – and Henry McGee was interviewing him and the Chinese man was talking about a forthcoming election and, of course, the Chinese man had that cartoon thing with his l's and r's, so he said that he was going to have an erection. McGee looked puzzled, a familiar childlike grin spread across the Chinese man's face, and a young lad's face went bright red as his father laughed and his mother said something about it being very rude. Later in the sketch there was some gag about how the Chinese man was having trouble with his r's, but by then it was too late. It's probably one of the least consequential gags Benny Hill ever did, and it's funny how these things stick in your head, but memories are like that.

Fast-forward about 25 years and I'm on a driving holiday in the South of France. Elly, my eldest daughter, had a tape of songs that she insisted on listening to. (And listening to. And listening to.) One side of the tape was what used to be called 'children's favourites' – 'Tie Me Kangaroo Down', Pinky & Perky, some Max Bygraves song about toothbrushes, and 'Ernie the Fastest Milkman in the West' – and it was a spooky thing, but my wife and I immediately started singing along and we both remembered all the words.

> I said you'll have it pasteurized cos pasteurized is best,
> She said 'Ernie I'll be happy if it comes up to my chest.'
> That tickled old Ernie
> And he drove the fastest milkcart in the West.

It's a funny thing about growing up. You just can't escape it.

Prologue

I'M not sure what it is with Benny Hill. This is the third book I've written about a classic British comedian (the other two, *Tommy Cooper: Just Like That* and *Morecambe & Wise: You Can't See the Join*, are available at all good bookshops. While we're here, if you're interested in a book about Spurs . . .), and if we're going to look at this as some sort of quest, then I've got to be honest: I'm no nearer the truth. Tommy Cooper and Eric Morecambe were touched by something that I'm not sure we can ever get near. They had a spectral quality that simply made people laugh. You can say the words 'Tommy Cooper' to anyone, and if they've even seen him just once they'll smile that smile of warm recognition. Tommy could just stand there – not do anything, just stand there – and that would be enough. Similarly Eric Morecambe. Whatever it was he had, he had it in buckets. This is a man who could move his glasses a quarter of an inch off the centre of his nose and do nothing else and make an audience cry. Ernie Wise, too, was in his way something special. First, for a showman he was amazingly devoid of ego, itself a miracle in this business. He was content to let Eric get the laughs, get the plaudits to the extent where he was almost invisible. But he was the best straight man there ever was. And ask any comedian, any actor, that is a gift just like any other. And Benny Hill?

I'm not sure what it is with Benny Hill. What it was about him, about his humour, that touched so many souls. Listen, of course all the comics we're talking about had exquisite timing and perfect judgement – we take that sort of stuff, the technical side of things, for granted – but they all had a comic presence that existed over and above the simple fact of their material. Where the true comedy greats are concerned, whether it's Eric Morecambe or Groucho Marx, the material in itself is almost incidental. It's something else. For the most part, this was Tommy Cooper:

'Doctor, you've got to help me. It hurts when I go like that.'
(He lifts his arm up)
Doctor: 'Well, don't do that.'

While the studio audience were laughing like drains, and I was still trying to work it out, Cooper rummaged around a table-top strewn with what looked like jumble sale tat and found a joke pair of glasses that had a pair of plastic antlers attached. He put them on. 'Horn-rimmed glasses.'

Eric Morecambe had a bag of catchphrases that he repeated (and repeated and repeated), but rarely got a bigger laugh than when he looked at the camera and made an idiot grin. He would make references to Ernie's wig, he'd say, 'What do you think of it so far?' and then do a bit of stupid ventriloquism: 'Ruggish.'

And Benny Hill? Benny Hill outsold them all. He went round the world. He conquered America so far into the heartland that people had car stickers saying things like, 'I'm watching Benny Hill.' People threw Benny Hill parties. TV stations had not just Benny Hill nights but Benny Hill weekends. He was a proper phenomenon. And why? When people look back and think of Benny Hill, the image that sticks is those old speeded-up chases at the end of his shows. 'Yakety Sax' playing as Benny chased little Jackie Wright, slapping his bald head as they were both chased by a bevy of semi-clad lovelies. Was that it? Was that what made him probably the most popular comic in the world? Was it really that he put semi-naked women in his shows? Was it really that he appealed to the lowest common denominator? If we can look at Cooper and Morecambe and say 'instinct', if we can look at Wise and say 'sublime comic talent', what can we say when we look at Benny Hill? What are we going to do? Point to Fred Scuttle? Mr Chow Mein? The Hill's Angels?

Benny Hill was, for 40 years, the most popular comic in Britain. For about half that time he was probably the most popular comic in the world. Yet he died alone, cast aside like his shows. It seems inconceivable looking back now. He made Thames TV . . . Well, I was going to say he made Thames TV loads of money, but the sentence is probably more accurate if we just leave it as 'he made Thames TV', yet it acted like it was almost ashamed of him. In his later years he did some questionable things, wrote some sketches and made some of what we can, if we're feeling charitable, call lapses of judgement. Sketches like the rape sketch. Sketches like this: a cowboy chances upon a fair maiden tied to a railway line. From the state of her dress it's obvious that she's been raped. Benny (the cowboy) looks to the camera, gives it that familiar leer, that leer of the naughty schoolboy looking at a dirty mag, and says to her 'This really isn't your lucky day' as he reaches for his trousers. Think back now and you wonder quite how that happened. But before you condemn him for it, remember this. He might have written it, but a TV station broadcast it and a viewing public created the climate for him to perform it. It wasn't me, Your Honour. It was the era. It's the same with the other stuff, the non-girlie stuff. Much of it was outrageously racist. Mr Chow Mein's humour was almost entirely based on linguistic misunderstandings. It's all very well Hill saying that the joke was on the English-speaking viewers because 'How many people can speak Mandarin as well as he speaks English?' but that argument is, frankly, borrocks. The gags are based on him not being able to speak English. That's it, and for Benny to start quoting the Ironic Defence is not going to wash. There were too many sketches featuring mean Jews and thick Irishmen knocking around. Were they jokes on the audience's perceptions too?

There's another salient point to make about Benny Hill. Comics like Morecambe and Wise were geniuses. We've had that conversation and we agree. But even though they were geniuses, they were also blessed in that they had great writers working for them. Eddie Braben, Sid Green and Dick Hills … great writers. With the exception of a short period in the early Sixties when Dave Freeman collaborated with him, Benny Hill did it all himself. The vision, the execution . . . it was all his own.

There are so many obvious ironies, so many strange sadnesses. Benny Hill, a man who was arguably the most successful – that's to say the most popular – comedian of the postwar era, died alone in his flat in Teddington, and when he died his body lay there for two days before anyone discovered it. Without labouring the point, think about that for a moment. He died alone, and that's fair enough. You live alone, you die alone. You create the conditions for your life. But it was two days before anyone knew. That's two days with no one noticing he was gone. Two days when no one phoned up. Two days when no one popped round. That's the sad part, the sad aspect of it all. No housekeeper even. Nothing.

'People were wrong to feel sad because Benny died alone and his body lay undiscovered for two days,' says Sue Upton, the head girl Hill's Angel. 'Although I am devastated by his death, I don't feel sad about the way he went because it was perfect for him. He died watching TV, which was his absolute favourite pastime, and suddenly without any suffering.'

'A master comic and one of the funniest men to grace the television.'
Bob Hope

When looking at Benny Hill, you've got to look back at the whole story. You can't simply focus on the sad fat man of the latter years and say, 'That's Benny Hill.' The

Aged 15 Benny became a milkman. He really did drive the fastest milkcart in the west

thing to always remember with Benny Hill is this: you don't get to be the most famous comedian in, arguably, the world if you're not something absolutely special. You can fool some of the people some of the time, remember? Benny's humour cut through language and nationality, through culture and history. Yet today it seems a very long way away. Morecambe and Wise seem locked in time, maybe because of the guests they had and maybe because of the clothes they wore – terrible suits and elephant collars. Tommy Cooper, too, seems locked in time because he's so quintessentially music hall. He's the only comic from that era who survived and translated to the small screen, the only television-era comic who was essentially a 'turn'. Benny it's the time rather than the person that's locked. It's the mid-1970s, the world of Mannikin cigars, Cossack hairspray, dodgy sitcoms. We can laugh an ironic laugh at the hair and the Brut ads and the Denim ads and the men who don't have to try too hard, but really it was a grim old time, a time just waiting for Johnny Rotten and the rest to kick it out.

The curious fact about him – and maybe this says more about everyone else than it does about him – is that he was most successful when he was least innovative, when he was most staid and dull. Yes, when he was cutting-edge he was popular, but it was nothing compared to the later Thames years. Whose fault is that?

'Nobody else has created such excellence for the small screen, which is why I believe that when the postwar period is assessed, Benny Hill's will be the only name to join the pantheon of great comedians.'
Michael Bentine in the late 1950s

Chapter 1 From Benny to Ben

IT was the sort of gag that Benny would have played on Jack Wright. It was one of those gags that was cruel and, if it wasn't played on you, it would have been tragically funny. Benny Hill is a man who has been frozen in our thoughts as a television anachronism, a fossil in his own lifetime, but what had secured his position in the first place was his eye for innovation, his ability to stay ahead of the crowd, his way of seeing what the future held and getting there first.

Hill is often called the first comedian made by television, and like everything, it's true and it's not true. Television made him more famous, but television made everyone who was famous more famous. Hill started out in a remarkably conventional way, made his mark in a conventional way, and established himself with more of the same. It's just that like all the people we remember best, he did it more successfully than most.

It's been said that Benny Hill was nothing more than an updated version of Max Miller. A less rude version – Max Miller lite. Max Miller crossed with Donald McGill. And that was maybe true, certainly for a while anyway. When he ran away to London, aged seventeen, with nothing but a few bob in his pocket, he looked like a junior podgy version of Miller with his loud comedy suits and his blue material. But come on. Be fair. He was seventeen, fresh out of Southampton. He was looking for big city streets, for golden pavements. No, the Miller fixation came and went fairly quickly, and as soon

as his fame gave him a chance to breathe and take a few chances, he ditched it. Much of his work was ahead of the game. The studio trickery and the technical advances, we'll go into detail about that later. But just consider some of the material here, not how it was presented or how it was engineered. Look at this sketch from 1957:

A man walks into a taxidermist's to have a duck stuffed. The taxidermist's assistant doesn't know the story and eats the duck. The taxidermist gets hold of a dead parrot and tries to pass it off as the duck.

Customer: It's gone a funny colour, hasn't it?
Taxidermist: Yes, I'm afraid that happens sometimes. It's the steaming, you see, sir. We have to steam them before you stuff them.
Customer: But its beak is a different shape.
Taxidermist: Well, sir, that's the shrinkage. It shrinks, you see, when we apply the embalming fluids.
Customer: But it looks like a parrot.
Taxidermist: Yes, it does a bit, doesn't it? Now that you mention it.

Any similarity to a sketch performed in the mid-1970s by a fêted comedy troupe is purely coincidental.

Hill was 28 when he did that. The following year, in 1958, an internal BBC memo to Ronnie Waldman, head of Light Entertainment, said this: 'Subject: *The Benny Hill Show*, Saturday 1 February 1958. This, I thought, was in places brilliant. At the same time I am always worried that Hill will say or do something unacceptable.' Most young comics would give their right arm to have a memo like that written about them. It says that you're everything that a young comic should be: brilliant, funny, sharp and dangerous. What more could you want? That, at the time, everything in the memo was true, that was the nice thing.

In the late 1950s, Benny Hill was about as cutting-edge as it gets. Looking back, thinking back now, that's a curious notion, no? In the days when Benny first started to make proper inroads into the world of television, it was a Reithian nightmare. There was a list of forbidden words and forbidden subjects. Vicars were off the menu. Words like 'knickers' weren't allowed. The Goons got away with Hugh Jampton, but only because none of the BBC Brahmins spent time in the ranks. A honeymoon wasn't considered fair game. Any sort of speech impediment, that was out. Television producers grabbed performers who'd grown up in the music halls, who'd learnt their trade on the stage, but then they expected them to suddenly change their acts and become, I don't know, something out of *The Brady Bunch*, washed, brushed and manicured.

Benny Hill was smart and he was lucky. Lucky because he was the right age at the right time, smart because he saw it. In terms of the development of Britain's television age, Benny Hill appeared at exactly the right time. As the 1950s turned into the 1960s and the 1960s turned into the 1970s, we were one nation united by a television screen. This was the era of three-channel television. No Channel 4, no Channel 5. Cables were still attached to wirelesses, satellites only existed in James Bond films, and Rupert Murdoch was selling advertising space on the *Darwin Gazette* . . .

We were on the cusp of what was and what was to come. Television was now accessible to all, and cheap enough to be a true mass medium. It was no longer a mystery, reserved for a privileged few. Nearly every household had a television, and the days when people would gaze in wonder as the white spot disappeared at the end of the day had long gone. Yet it wasn't so cheap that families had more than one set. There wasn't a question of little Johnny disappearing up to his room to watch *Alien Death Zone* on Sky's new Zombie TV channel. If little Johnny wanted to watch telly, he watched what his parents watched.

How many of us grew up sitting around the television as a family watching Benny Hill, getting to know him, his characters, his gags . . . All as a family. It captured a cross-generation audience in a way that would simply not be possible now, and it united people in a way that simply does not happen any more. I can't remember how many people I've talked to, contemporaries, who when I've mentioned that I was writing a book about Hill said something like 'Yeah, I was around, I watched it.' You watched it (and no disrespect here) because there was nothing else to watch. Looking back, it was a gentler time, a time when things were a little less frenetic, a little less rushed. We were united. In fairness, it's probably all dewy-eyed nostalgic nonsense, but that's the way it seems and so that's the way it was.

It enabled comics like Hill (and Morecambe and Wise) to build an audience and pull in 20 million viewers, something that would be inconceivable today. It enabled them to become not so much television stars as cultural icons. It also made them enormously powerful within the corporations that employed them: there was a period at Thames when Benny Hill was the golden goose, in more senses than one. And that was before he cracked America. His success gave him free rein, and too much power isn't good for anyone. What Benny said ruled. No one said No. The control mechanisms went – well, out of control, over the top, as we said a bit later.

And that's how it was with Benny. His whole life was like the diet of a binge eater, but maybe that's not so surprising, given that his whole life was lived that way. When things went well they went seriously well. But when things started to go wrong, they went seriously disastrous. People went for his comedy – fair game – but they also went for his life, and that confused him. And for a man who's already confused about how the world works . . . that's ultra-confusing.

The story goes that Ben Elton killed Benny Hill and, yes, it was Elton's interview in 1986 that acted as the catalyst for the chain of events that would see Hill sacked so unceremoniously in 1989. (Elton said that he could find nothing funny in Benny Hill's little old man chasing girls round the park when the incidence of rape was up and it was unsafe for women to be in parks at night.) Benny couldn't understand that. Where he came from – in his world – you simply didn't do that. Knocking other comedians simply wasn't done. It was bad manners. You could be as rude as you liked (or as rude as you could get away with), but bad manners was against the rules he knew. But then again, there wasn't much about that time that Benny understood. In the late 1980s when the anti-Hill criticism was at its peak and the vultures were circling overhead, he sat down and watched Billy Connolly, counted the expletives and scratched his head. 'They can say that, but if I tell a girl "Your dumplings are boiling over" everybody shouts "Filth!" I don't know why.'

In truth Hill's demise started long before Ben Elton got in on the act. His ratings might have been up, up, up, but his personality profile was going down, down, down. When your head is above the parapet, when you live in the public eye, and especially when you've made your name by being ahead of the rest, you've got to stay out there in front. That's the way life is. But it's a curious thing. You've got to be constantly dancing, never stop moving your feet, or else you're going to get burned. Make a step today, and if you're still there tomorrow they'll see you and they'll shoot you down. But you've got to do it delicately, with the grace of a ballet dancer, for if you do it clumsily they'll see you and they'll shoot you all the same. That, essentially, is what happened to

He rarely got the girl. With Jane Novello and friend, 1958

Benny Hill. He got shot down because he didn't move: not quickly enough, not at all.

Also, you've got to remember, things were changing. Racism had had its day. The Black and White Minstrels had been canned in 1986. Bimbo sexism was also in trouble and Miss World was on the way out. The old-fashioned, too, was under attack, and in the same period *Dr Who* found himself lost in space. This was the era of MTV, a time when the non-terrestrial channels were beginning to make inroads. Television was beginning to shape up and was about to undergo the biggest shake-up since ITV started, since telly went technicolor. Even without taking into account the Hill's Angels questions and the Ben Elton interviews, Benny Hill was looking strictly last century, daddy-o.

Looking back, armed with a bag full of hindsight, I'm not even sure that it was the 'birds' and the 'bristols', the girls with their dumplings, that did for him. Listen, his television career didn't take off in isolation. It took off as the whole television culture went into orbit. Television stars weren't like movie stars or American rock'n'roll stars or sports stars or anything else – mysterious characters who moved in a different world. And they weren't like the radio stars of the old days – disembodied voices. They were real. Television stars, telly people, were accessible. They were in your living room. They were our friends. And because they were our friends, we wanted to know about them. The more we knew, the more we wanted to know. It wasn't quite *Hello!* but it was the start. And the biggest star was Benny Hill, and what did we know about him? About as much as we know now. Zip.

Tongues started wagging, stories started spreading, and because there was nothing to back any of it up, the stories stuck. For a start, Benny wasn't married. Doesn't matter that he came out with all that 'Why buy a book when you can join a library' shtick, he wasn't married, and our society had a tendency to go into nudge-nudge, wink-wink overdrive when a man fails to meet the matrimonial deadline. It happened to Ted Heath in the 1970s and it happened to Benny Hill. Poor old Ted Heath played music and went sailing. Benny spent much of the late 1950s – well, a lot of time on the telly anyway – in drag. And not surprisingly he was good at it. Hang about. A man dresses up as a woman and he's not married? Are you quite sure?

Back in the late 1950s when all this started, Benny was still sharp, but crucially he made the wrong decision. He thought that if he took off the dresses and started talking about football, everyone would think he was a real man. Faced with what he thought was the choice of either spiritually inviting journalists into his lovely home and seeing how he really lived, or changing, he changed. Out went the drag characters, out went the effeminate catchphrase 'Bless your hearts', and in came the lecherous old geezers. Benny never did catch on. The rules don't change. If you don't tell people anything, they're not going to get bored and go away, or be happily fobbed off with a few mock macho one-liners. They're only ever going to want to know more.

If only he'd been so receptive to change in the 1970s. But maybe by then it was too late. By then he'd become too successful. Maybe he thought that he was fireproof. He was Benny Hill, he'd been at the top ever since he started trying. When people started knocking him . . . how could they be right? He was still pulling in millions of viewers, still selling across the globe. These critics, how could they be right and everyone else be wrong? It's like when he was criticized by Mary Whitehouse for making what she called soft porn. 'She is after all just one viewer,' he said. 'I always ask myself who will be offended. If a lot are, then forget it.'

I suppose that up to a point he was right. People had been making noises about his use of women almost since he started performing. But he grew up with the Max Miller generation. All he was doing was making visual what the Millers of the world were talking about. As Miller might have said, 'What should he do? Go back the way he came or toss himself off?'

The problem for Benny was that by the time a lot of people started to express how they were offended, it was too late. He was too old, too set in his ways. And, you know, we're just animals really. When an animal gets too old to keep up, too slow to adapt to a new environment . . . it gets eaten.

Did Benny Hill deserve to get eaten?

Chapter 2 Ready Rubbed

YOU can't talk about any cultural phenomenon without placing it in the context of its time, and despite the sexual advances of the 1960s – it's a curious thing, but if I were writing about any other subject, I'm sure I'd have written 'Despite the advances made in the 1960s . . .', but here I am writing about Benny Hill, and it's funny how the sexual innuendo just rolls off the fingertips. You're lucky you can't see me writing this – in all probability I'd be throwing you the odd leer. Anyway, where were we? Despite the sexual advances of the 1960s, criticisms that the show was sexist were greeted with 'So what?' shrugs. Even the term used – Women's Lib – had a comic air to it.

Benny Hill was so much a creature of his time. He came from a family steeped in the entertainment industry. He grew up in a world where variety was accessible, where it was possible for a young boy to fulfil his dreams. Even going into the army was contemporary. Frankie Howerd was there. Ian Carmichael. All the boys from Bob Monkhouse to Peter Sellers. He came out and television was waiting, gift-wrapped like a postwar present. Every time he was ready to make another step, the world was right there.

Now, spin back to the 1970s. The 1970s really were a long time ago. If, through some Wellsian time warp, you could have placed a 1996 edition of *FHM* magazine back in 1973 you'd have had the Obscene Publications people on your back. Back in

It was always schoolboy humour. . . with Vivienne Martin, 1960

1973, even the *Playboy*s and *Mayfair*s didn't look like that. Things had a little more mystery. These were the days of the catalogue, days when young boys found out what was what and where was where by looking at the underwear section. And don't suppose that it was only in our house that the Green Shield Stamp album was well-thumbed on the page that advertised showers. And don't tell me that it was coincidence that those showers were advertised by slinky women who were pictured carefully washing themselves, showing just that curve of breast and expanse of thigh.

The majority of the television comedies of the time were really no better and no worse than Benny Hill. *Man About the House*. The *Doctor* series. *Please Sir!*. *On The Buses*. *Father Dear Father*. While they might not have been so reliant on acres of flesh, and while they might not have had such unsavoury characters as Hill's, they were still rooted in the casual sexism and racism of the time. It's important to remember that, for all the talk of the Permissive Sixties or the Swinging Sixties, for all the talk of Women's Liberation, this was still a very dark time for women and women's rights.

The adverts of the day displayed flesh levels that today we would find hard to believe, let alone accept. The Manikin cigar adverts stick in the mind particularly. A woman dressed in a skimpy bikini goes running through a jungle. Her bikini snags on a branch and gets ripped off. The woman runs along, holding her breast with maybe one hand (the other is holding the cigars). There was one classic I remember where the woman did all this and then her bikini bottom got caught . . . You probably get the idea. St Bruno. You remember the St Bruno ad? A Milk Tray man is followed by hundreds of gorgeous chicks. He stops and turns to his minder, gets him to wave one of them through. Then the pay-off line   St Bruno was 'ready-rubbed'. You know, I never knew whether that was meant as a gag. Cigar adverts were particularly conspicuous, but it was an attitude that spread through the whole of British culture. Remember the *Top of the Pops* record compilations? Remember their covers? To call their clothes skimpy is to give the impression the cover girls were wearing sheepskin coats. They weren't even approaching skimpy. Maybe they had on a crocheted tea cosy. Maybe.

It was a time when that strange phenomenon called soft porn was at its height. While the rest of the world opened up, the parental British authorities, led by the tightly bound God-slot campaigner Mary Whitehouse, banned real pornography from these shores. Sometimes it's so nice to have the choice taken away from you, though it's perhaps fortunate that Mrs Whitehouse wasn't too encouraged by her successes. Who knows where that might have led?

No sex please, we're British. Anyway, the upshot of our guardians' good work was soft porn. It would have been less than a step away from those 1950s *Playboy*s with the public, sorry, pubic hair airbrushed out, had it not been for that other great British invention, saucy humour. Double entendres, wordplays featuring key words like 'come' and 'up', and bagfuls of so-bad-they're-funny jokes. Mix and match Donald McGill's seaside postcards, the *Carry On* films, Frankie Howerd, Max Miller, and then add liberal doses of naked girls. No boys' bits, you understand – why, the sight of them would probably make you go blind.

It sounds crap, but for a few short years, soft porn was glorious in a way only the Brits can contrive. A genre came and went in, maybe, five years. Like all genres, it created its own environment, its own language and its own stars. And in the world of soft porn, few stars shone brighter than Fiona Richmond. Legend has it she was a 'normal' housewife in a previous life before being born again as Fiona, one of those chesty girls with an all-round tan who never travel by plane. Allegedly. Fiona's car had the number plate FU 2. Soft porn was respectable. Proper actors appeared in the films. Proper British character actors, people like Benny's stooge Bob Todd. *The Adventures of a Handyman. The Confessions of a Window Cleaner.* Brushed denim flares, Cortinas, and young starlets running around with their kit off. Maybe you'd get the girl from *Please Sir!* (And while we're here, what about *Please Sir!*? How near did that get to setting up a new genre, paedophilia sitcom? Sexy schoolgirls and dirty old teachers.) The soft-porn films were fantastically successful for, maybe, three years, during which time they upped the ante and all but killed off the *Carry On* films. Who wanted to see Barbara Windsor pretend to lose her bra when they could see Linda Hayden's publics?

Benny was aware of all that. If he was to keep his edge, he had to stay ahead of the game. If they were doing that in the cinema, what could he get away with on the telly? And listen, this new style had put a lot of his old contemporaries (the *Carry On* types) out of work. He wasn't going to let that happen to him. And he wasn't the only one. It didn't take Frankie Howerd long to get his toga out.

Talking about the culture of the time, there's one other point which we can make here. What do the names Julia Breck, Carol Cleveland and Cleo Rocos mean to you? Anything? No, they probably don't. In Benny Hill's defence we should point out that those great gods of British comedy, Monty Python, used to pepper their sketches with liberal doses of Carol Cleveland, a possibly lovely woman, a woman who possibly was a great comic actress, but a woman whom the Python boys wouldn't let do anything except walk around with precious few clothes on. Similarly Julia Breck. She was Spike Milligan's version. Sketches in his Q series would often end abruptly with Julia Breck walking on set flashing the most enormous breasts you ever did see. Again, like Cleveland, she didn't get to say anything, she didn't get to do anything apart from flash her enormous breasts. Cleo Rocos was Kenny Everett's. Same story.

Kenny Everett used Cleo Rocos. Monty Python used Carol Cleveland. Spike Milligan used Julia Breck. We can argue all day long about the situation, about the ways in which they were used, the ways in which they were portrayed, and you know all those arguments are valid enough. We can intellectually justify them all, we can play with them, we can dissect them. But the fact remains that what those comics were doing was using a semi-naked woman to pull in the punters. Listen. They might have all been fine comic actors, but do you seriously think that Rocos, Cleveland or Breck would have found such ready employment had they been the proud owners of a 32A bust? If any of them hadn't had breasts the size of Venezuela, they wouldn't have got the job. What Benny Hill did, was it any worse? He objectified women, he used women, he treated them as breasts on legs. Before considering that, consider this. Milligan came from the intellectually feted Goons. Monty Python, we all know, are very clever university chaps. Everett came through via the hipper-than-hip world of pirate radio. Benny Hill came through the very working class University Of Life – variety, music hall, that kind of thing. It's only an idea, but is this a bit of class bias we can detect here? The subversive, hip, educated BBC intellectuals against Hill, the consummate ITV light entertainer, a working-class oik making working-class shows for the working class.

While we're here, it's worth pointing out that Everett, Milligan and the Pythons were all, like Hill, capable of writing comedy sketches that were, if not racist, then certainly xenophobic. Yet no one has ever criticized them in the way that they've criticized Hill, no one has pilloried them, they haven't been cast out. But I don't know. Maybe all that really shows is that Everett, Milligan and the Pythons were all a whole barrel of apples smarter than Benny Hill.

Chapter 3 Loaded

Tell me. In an age when it's deemed acceptable for FHM *magazine to project a huge image of TV presenter Gail Porter's naked body on the side of the Houses of Parliament, why do people still recoil when you mention the name Benny Hill?*

IT'S a curious thing, but why is it that Benny Hill hasn't been resurrected? What is it about him that frightens people off? OK, I can understand why he was banished to the Political Correctness sin bin when he was, but why is it he hasn't been rescued? Why wasn't he rehabilitated by the post-irony brigade who spent the best part of the 1990s dragging previously discarded cultural icons out of the broom cupboard and declaring them newly hip? Once upon a time, Frankie Howerd (who Benny was linked to, from the army unit they shared to the same Easter weekend they both died on) couldn't get arrested. But then he got the post-irony treatment and, what do you know? Full houses. There were stacks of people who were similarly rehabilitated – you can take a handful of the *Carry On* crew for starters – people who had been exiled but came back peddling essentially the same rubbish but with a knowing sideways grin. Sometimes it seemed that the more crass the basic model, the more scope there was for rehabilitation. But while countless crass, cheesy singers and comics were blessed with new post-ironic leases of life, no one came knocking on Benny Hill's door. Why?

It's a question that is even more perplexing when you look back at the 1990s. What goes around comes around. Fashions and tastes and styles are cyclical – if you're out of fashion the only thing you can be sure of is that one day soon you'll be back in. Refined, reconditioned, restructured even, but back. So while it might be true that much of the 1980s was concerned with notions of political correctness and an almost Stalinist zeal in purging what was seen as unacceptable, the truth was that however thorough the purge was, what it would be followed by would be equally thorough. Black follows white follows black follows white. You know those executive toys where you've got five balls hanging down and if you bounce a ball at one end the one at the other bounces off a similar distance? Cause and effect. That's the way it happens.

And thus it was that as an era, the mid-1990s were as sexist a time as I can recall, with shows that revelled in their smutty schoolboy sniggers. The more risqué the humour got, the more the viewers tuned in. The more blatant it got, the higher the ratings rose. The more sexist it got, the louder the critics applauded.

Elsewhere in British culture, the advent of cheap sexism was even more emphatic. It was called 'laddism', but what it really was was just good old trusty sexism. The old faithful. Donald McGill with better technology and cruder gags. The rise of comics like *Loaded*, *FHM*, *Esquire*, *GQ*, *Maxim* and *Later* was the revenge of sexism on a nightmarish scale. Containing enough female flesh to almost kill dead the older top-shelf magazines like *Playboy* and *Men Only*, these 'style mags' took sexism on to a new level, relying exclusively on getting top telly starlets to display their 'charms'. Every month one of these magazines would up the ante, and every month the others would have to follow. While we're at it, last weekend (that's May 2000 to you historians) the *Guardian* newspaper carried a full-page colour advert with the headline 'At last an oven even men can use'. Sometimes you have to wonder whether anything has changed at all.

Much of what the PC lobby were arguing against was, in truth, indefensible. Looking back now, who's seriously going to argue in favour of shows like *Love Thy Neighbour*? If you watch the stand-up comedy of the day, much of it was abhorrent. *Please Sir!* was a gag – great characters, but don't you think it fetishized schoolgirls just a little bit? (Actually, now I'm thinking about Britney Spears. Maybe *Please Sir!* was just ahead of its time.) Try watching television shows of the day now, shows like *Wheeltappers*. Take out all the sexism and racism, prune all the gags about 'my wife'

and 'the mother-in-law', and what you'd have left would be an advert break.

The irony – and we're talking about proper irony here, not that lame post-irony nonsense – is that the sexism of the 1990s was far worse, far more aggressive and 'serious' than the sexism of Benny Hill's age. If you were an actress or a telly presenter you had to get your kit off. There were no two ways about it. You had to do the publicity for your new show, and if you wanted to do the publicity you had to get your kit off. If you were a wannabe – an actress or a telly presenter on the make – there was simply no choice. Women were objectified as they'd never been before, and there was no question of control, of power, of who was in the driving seat. For those 'perfect body' types, maybe they can feel comfortable doing it. But what if you didn't have that 'perfect body'? What if you didn't feel comfortable? What if you were . . . say it quietly . . . fat? It doesn't matter. This sort of sexism lacks compassion, despises understanding.

Take your clothes off or else . . . no job.

And the humour. What is the difference between comedian Rory McGrath making some geezer gag and Benny Hill making some schoolboy gag about dumplings? McGrath's gags are far more aggressively sexist, full of a disdain and an anger that Hill never had. I'm not even going to go near the question of 'Is it funny?' I'm just saying, what's the difference? What's the difference between Benny Hill being chased by a bevy of blonde, buxom Hill's Angels and smart, chic *GQ* magazine having a near-naked telly starlet on its cover?

On one level it might seem that there's no difference. It's all sexist. It's all men using women's bodies to sell a product and, yes, in so many ways that's indefensible. It's not something that I'm going to argue for, but it is what it is. There's no point getting all King Canute about it. Women's bodies are attractive. We all – men and women – like looking at them. As far back as I can remember, things have been sold on the back of women's flesh. From Hollywood to the stage to the television, the entertainment business has traded on women. If you look at the darkest corner of a Neanderthal cave I dare say you'll find a faded image of some Stone Age Gail Porter lying suggestively on a mammoth skin. No one can argue against the effectiveness of that tactic. It's been going on since before time began, and to start denying it now makes no sense at all.

This fairly straightforward reversal of the pendulum is typical of the way Brits do things. Go wildly over the top one way and then react with equal force the other way. A brief look at the television guide for tonight (Thursday, 11 May 2000) gives us two programmes that would put Dear Old Benny in a tailspin if he were still alive.

10.40 pm *X Certificate* – A review of the latest adult film and video releases.

11.10 pm *European Blue Review* – Featuring nude house cleaners.

Huh? People get all of a lather about Benny Hill and his dumplings gags, and programmes like that are available? Listen, I should have said. Those two programmes weren't on some iffy cable channel. It was what my mother would call proper television. OK, so they're on reasonably late, while Benny was on at 8pm, family time. It's fair to say, but still. 10.40pm isn't that late, and, it might sound strange, but I've got a sneaky suspicion that if they put Benny Hill on instead of *European Blue Review* they'd still get a few raised eyebrows.

But Benny Hill hasn't been resurrected, and if what was in the last 1,000 words or so was the simple truth, if it is true that it was just Hill's sexism that people found unpalatable, that would be inexplicable. Given that we don't deal in the inexplicable – if you want inexplicable, go read a book on the Loch Ness Monster – we've got to look elsewhere. So what is it about him that frightens people off?

Chapter 4 The Unacceptable Face

THINK about Benny Hill. Think of the classic end-of-show skit, the speeded-up chase with 'Yakety Sax' playing. The sketch that's your idea of a typically sexist Benny Hill sketch. Benny's looking at a group of semi-clad women. He's leering at them and ogling them and fantasizing about them and looking at the camera – at us – conspiratorially, inviting us into his head. What would he only like to do to them. What was he going to do? Such a stud. Such a man. Those poor women. Little do they know. Suddenly . . . they see him. They turn on him. They're chasing him away. Cue speeded-up film and Benny Hill music. Now think of a glossy men's magazine cover. The siren with her bits hanging out and her come-hither eyes. She's begging you to come closer, to hold her, to pick her up. To buy her.

The classic Case for the Defence is this: In the Benny Hill sketch the women are the ones with the power. He has been leering, but as soon as they see him they turn. *They* chase *him*. They chase him off. Numerically, spiritually and physically, the women are stronger. In the case of the magazine cover, the women are passive. The men have got the power. The men have the power to buy the women. So listen, which is the more exploitative?

That's the defence, the argument that's put forward by Hill's supporters. It's a case that revolves around the question of power. Who has it? The question of who has

the power is seen as key in considering notions of exploitation. 'Everyone knows that it's the girls who are chasing Benny' is an argument you hear time and time again.

How many Hollywood films through the ages have been based around the simple premise of a man chasing a pretty girl? And in how many of those films has the man been old enough to be the girl's father? It's a staple, something we have all grown to accept as normal. An older man chasing a young girl, a young girl who, more often than not, falls for the man. Even if she doesn't fall for him, she finds him attractive. Cute. Charming. Attractive. Now then. You don't need a diploma in feminist theory to understand why this is such a popular image. Who are the producers? Who are the directors? Who are the stars? Older men, all of them, and what we see on the screen is largely those old men's fantasies. Yes, I might be bald and fat, I might have bad breath, I might have seen the last of my beauty, but I'm still attractive enough to be a babe magnet.

Forget for a minute whether that is an acceptable scenario. It's an established image, a plot we feel comfortable with. You see that and you don't bat an eye. In those Hollywood films the man might be older but he's invariably good-looking, sophisticated, witty and charming. Even Woody Allen, someone's who's traded on the old man/young woman dynamic more than most, is acceptable because he's intellectually attractive.

What Benny Hill did was very nearly the same – but it wasn't the same. It was something darker, more troubling, more subversive. Not only is the Benny Hill character much older than the women, he isn't attractive in any way. He isn't a sophisticate, isn't good-looking, isn't in any conceivable way a hunk. He's fat and greasy and sweating. But there's something else. In the traditional scenario, the male is an adult, he's mature. Benny Hill's character is a child, a child trapped inside a man's body. It looks like a man – it's the right size and shape – but the body language is all wrong. The body language is childlike, like he's in a playground or maybe sneaking around the girls' changing rooms.

There's something about the character that makes you think that he's leering, a frisson of weird. Maybe he's wearing a mac or something. Where are his hands? What are they doing? Is he having a bit of a fiddle? It's uncomfortable. Suddenly, the character doesn't look so innocent. Could it be that the sketch isn't sexist at all, but something else altogether, something dirtier, something seedier, something that we don't really want to talk about and look at up close?

It's this leering aspect of Benny Hill's work that has held him back. Objectifying women is OK as long as you're doing it within the confines of what is expected, what is acceptable. And what is acceptable is to be sexist in a sophisticated way, because somehow that's adult. What Hill did – and this is perhaps why he's still living in pariah-land – was to not treat women the way an adult would treat them, or at any rate not a 'red-blooded' male adult. He had a childlike perspective, and when you put that perspective inside an adult's body and surround it with a bevy of semi-clad lovelies . . . it's a curiously uncomfortable mix.

It was another of Hill's misfortunes that the change in the socio-political climate coincided with his getting older. This is another thing Hill has in common with Woody Allen. If there's one thing less palatable than a young man running around chasing semi-clad young lovelies, it's an old man running around chasing semi-clad young lovelies.

'I never understand why I'm called a sexist. What does it mean? Girls on the beach with no bras? Madonna in her underwear? I don't monitor TV but within a month I've heard the female "c" word eleven times, and you can always see pictures of gentles with public hair. The first time BBC2 got great viewing figures was for Casanova, *and what was that? Wall-to-wall ladies' chest pimples. But if I tell a girl "Your dumplings are boiling over" everyone shouts "Filth!" I don't know why.'*

Maybe the clue to the real answer is in his own words. Gentles? Public hair? There's something strange going on here.

Chapter 5 Comedians Are Funny Geezers

'He had this habit of disappearing after a day's work. The rest of us would have a meal in the hotel or a drink in the club, but Benny would be off on his own. He was one of the shyest, quietest men I have ever met in my life. I'm sure he wasn't insecure. It was just his way.'

Michael Caine, Benny's co-star in *The Italian Job*

IT'S a cliché, but like all clichés it's born out of truth. Comedians are funny geezers. Benny Hill was funnier than most. He had more foibles than a well-stocked foible shop. He was a loner. He was mean. He was paranoid. He was a control freak. He was a child. His sexuality was . . . questioned. He lived in a cheap, shabby flat when he was a multi-millionaire. He had no friends. He died alone. He used to go on holidays to faraway countries. His sexuality was . . . questioned.

He was undoubtedly an odd bloke, concerned with things that you or I might not have given a thought to. He was private to the point of paranoia. When the lease of his luxury Hyde Park flat came up for renewal, Benny decided that, no, he wouldn't renew it. Why not? There were builders working on the top-floor flat and, because it was a top-floor flat, they'd put up some scaffolding. Not unreasonable really. Well, not unless you were Benny. 'They [the builders standing on the scaffolding] might look in

Relaxing with Trudy Miller and a vey small glass of wine

one of my windows and see me with a girl. I can't have that.' So then he had to have somewhere to live, but that wasn't as easy for Benny as it might have been for someone with, how shall we say, a less keenly developed sense of insecurity. 'If I have a house it'll have to have a garden, and then I'll have to have a gardener who might sell a story to the papers about women he has seen me with. So I'd rather not.'

In later years, he lived in a flat in Teddington. By all accounts it was spare and Spartan and showed no outward signs of a personality having been imposed on it. It was, though, like a fortress designed to keep public eyes out and private life in, and he was reluctant to let anyone set foot inside it. He was far too clever and far too experienced to ever give anything away. In all the research I've done for this book there's nothing I've come across that gives any closer insight, that really looks behind the armour. I've lost count of the number of times I read him saying something like 'I don't know why you're asking me all this. I'm just a very ordinary, boring, normal guy.' There's plenty of deflective gags, plenty of transparent lies and plenty of blanks, but there's nothing that's open and honest and from the heart. And maybe that's OK, maybe people like me and you should leave it at that and not look for clues, not dig for the truth behind the public face.

Libby Roberts, a dancer with Hill from 1972 to 1975 and his choreographer from 1982 to 1989, said, 'Certainly Benny was an extremely private person who liked to be alone. He was a mystery man who didn't like his privacy invaded. He could chat to you for ages on the phone, but you would never turn up on his doorstep unannounced.' That's OK. I know people like that, but Benny was a star, a celebrity, and a personal space isn't allowed. We live in the age of a thousand glossy magazines called *Something With An Exclamation Mark!* and they're all full of two-bob celebs eager and happy to show us around their lovely homes and their lovely lives: I'll do anything to be on TV. Benny Hill came from a different era, a different age. The world he grew up into was a world where stars were altogether less accessible, where they had an allure, a sheen of mystery. The stories we could go into about people like Randolph Scott, David Niven, Errol Flynn . . . They're stories we all know bits of – or think we know bits of – but it's mostly conjecture, because stars back then didn't welcome you into their lovely homes.

And it wasn't only his public that didn't know him. His mother aside, he didn't get on with his family. His father was a bit of a brute. Harsh, emotionally violent, bitter.

Brutalized by the First World War, there wasn't a lot of room in his life for a podgy would-be thesp with a head full of dreams. Benny Hill didn't get on with his siblings. Well . . . when they were kids, Leonard Hill and Alfie Hill were best mates, but as they got older it all fell apart, so badly that they didn't speak for seventeen years. That's falling apart in style. What it was about is a bit of a mystery. Maybe a bit of jealousy, maybe some unfinished family business. Being the unknown brother of a famous person must be a terribly difficult thing to be. Any time somebody talks to you, what do they want? In his biography of his brother, *Saucy Boy*, Leonard, a teacher, confesses that as Benny got more and more successful it was too much of a burden to carry around. A key moment for Leonard was when he was given an unexpected promotion, and as he left the headmaster's office the head said, 'Oh, you will be able to get your brother to come down for the Christmas fête, won't you?' It must have been a bore. In 1989, Leonard decided enough was enough and rang up Benny. By all accounts, both were delighted to be back on terms. There was only ever his mother, Helen. Little Alfie (Benny's real name) loved his mother.

'Benny has always refused to dance to anyone else's tune,' said Bob Monkhouse. There's a story that Benny's long-time producer/associate Dennis Kirkland tells about the 1984 *Bring Me Sunshine* tribute show held at the London Palladium for Eric Morecambe. 'All the big comics were absolutely fascinated, gathered there to see Benny. They were in awe of him, not just because he's the most popular comedian in the world, but because they can't understand him. They don't know him socially, because he doesn't play golf with them, go to Stringfellow's or showbiz parties. He's a mystery man.' Maybe he just had different hobbies, went to different places.

Benny Hill was mean. That's the story. He was a multi-millionaire, but lived in a poky little flat. Later, when his beloved mother died, he moved into her house in Southampton. But he didn't change it, didn't decorate it, didn't repair it. What might seem like strange behaviour – OK, what *is* strange behaviour – can be explained very simply. His mother made him promise that he'd live there and wouldn't change it. He loved his mother and what she said, that was that. For the most part though, Benny had no understanding. It's the same with every other aspect of his life. He simply didn't view things as a grown adult might. When he was younger he was concerned about money. Of course he was. He came from a poor family and it mattered. If he didn't get some, no one was going to give it to him. But the older and more successful he got, the more he lost touch with what real things meant to real people.

He undoubtedly loved Sue Upton. In whatever way and from whatever distance, he loved her. He showered her kids with money and he promised her money but rarely delivered. It just wasn't in his head. The idea that he retreated to his little flat in Teddington and counted . . . It doesn't seem reasonable.

But you don't want to know about his paranoia, his meanness, his dysfunctional family relationships or what football team he supported (and growing up in Southampton must have been a heavy cross to bear). No. You want to know about the girls. You want to know about the sex.

Professionally, Benny Hill was surrounded by girls. They were his stooges, his set decoration, his props. They were the reason he came into the business. Benny Hill only became a comedian in the first place because he thought it would be a good way to meet women. 'As a kid I was showbiz daft. I used to go and watch review shows at the old Palace Theatre in Southampton, shows like *Ooh, You Saucy Girls*, *Ooh La La* and *Ici Paris*. They had to be cheeky or the local sailors wouldn't come in. There would be a string of pretty girls and a singer, but it was the comic who always caught my eye. I imagined he got all the birds – and was making a fortune at the same time. I thought that was the life for me.' Hill became interlinked with girls in the way that Eric Morecambe became interlinked with Ernie Wise and Ronnie did with Ronnie. But that was professionally. In his private life, things were very different.

He never married, and lived what you or I might consider a rather sad and lonely life. The more famous he got, the more the outside world was intrigued by his domestic 'status'. And the less they could find out, the more they thought they had a right to know. The longer it went on, the better the story became. And as with all men who live alone and don't invite the world in to have a nose, the word got round: Benny Hill was gay. (He'd soon take to calling himself, 'the only womanising poof in showbusiness'.)

Was it true? Truth shmuth, but what's truth in newspaperland? To Benny it was perplexing. He thought his heterosexuality, his fearsome manhood, was so obvious . . . how could anyone doubt it? When he was asked why he had never married, he would vary the reply, depending on whether the questioner was male or female. 'Why buy a book when you can join a library?' he'd say to a man. Or maybe, 'Why make one

Benny (centre with beer can) amid his 'extended family', the cast of his Show

woman miserable when I can make so many happy?' To a woman, he'd spin out the old tales like the one about having met and fallen in love with a married woman, or that he had his heart broken by a refusal.

Benny Hill was a funny bloke, for sure, and yet you can't help but feel that if you took the sexuality question out of the equation, no one would have made much fuss. But the sexuality question never would stay out of that equation. He would never confront it. He would never speak openly about it. What was he hiding? Libby Roberts said, 'Benny stayed in touch over the years, as he did with many of the girls on the show. However, we were only good friends and he never tried any funny business with me.' She added cryptically, 'If someone took his fancy it would invariably be a girl with a small bust.' Sue Upton said that if there was one of the Angels he fancied, he would ask her to sort it out. Mostly it was a lunch, but not always. There were a few of the dates that were a bit more nocturnal than that. 'I don't believe they were full relationships,' said Sue. 'I think he was celibate.'

So what was the woman story? Don't ask me. There are carrier bags full of unsubstantiated claims, and for the most part they're unsavoury and a little bit squalid. It's not a question of legal niceties and not wanting my fine publishers to get sued, but I just don't think it's worth going into. There are stories about the Hill's Angels and accounts of his trips abroad. Listen, if you're really interested you probably already know the tales, and if you don't know them and you want to find out I dare say there's some dodgy site on the Web that'll tell you (and if you ask it nicely it'll probably throw in a few 'celebrity nudes' for good measure). Benny never helped himself in this respect by never talking about it, never opening himself up for inspection.

What are the facts? These, gentlemen, are the facts. He proposed to Belinda Lee, but she refused. He proposed to two other dancers in the late 1950s, an Elaine and an Elizabeth. They both refused. By all accounts, the love of his life was the actress Annette André, who later made a bit of a name for herself as Marty's wife in *Randall & Hopkirk (Deceased)*. An Australian woman, Benny had met her during her years in service and offered an invitation to come over. She accepted that invitation. The next one he offered she didn't take up. The story goes that he was so heartbroken that he couldn't watch *Randall & Hopkirk* when it broke big.

'The sex in his private life was more innuendo than substance,' said his biographer Margaret Forwood. 'Benny decided love was too painful. It hurt too much when it went wrong, and in his case it usually did. Instead he established the image of the great Lothario practically fighting off girls . . . then he spent most of his time alone.' Bob Monkhouse said, 'Benny's relationships with girls have always been with younger women, not older, more demanding or mature women who would expect more from him perhaps than he wishes to give.'

I'm not in the game of making judgements about right and wrongs and about moral positions, just like I'm not in the game of reproducing unsubstantiated tabloid tittle-tattle. But he was a funny geezer. The more I read about Benny Hill, the more people I talked to and the more I found out, the more I became convinced. He was a funny geezer. I think he was just a bit odd, a bit not of this world. He was like a child both in his attitudes to money – 'Money isn't important. I was in Paris recently,' he said in 1991, 'and I thought "What can I spend it on?" I lunched three girls from the Crazy Horse. Two were from the north-east [of England] and I corresponded with one of them for a while but now she's gone to Tokyo. But what else can you do? Buy a nice shirt and a pair of socks?' – and in his attitudes to women.

Linguistically, he was an adolescent. Clive James, the TV critic of the *Observer* newspaper in the 1970s, was one of his big critics. Benny thought that 'Clive James has become synonymous for me with a bare boob. If you put a raspberry on top of his head you'd have one.' He spoke of gentles and publics and Bristols and boobies.It's playground-speak.

He had a reputation for being miserable, probably because he didn't play the celebrity game. But: 'I'm not miserable. And being well-known is no handicap. Imagine lying on a beach in St Tropez. A lovely lunch. A drink on the house, and three topless girls ask to have their pictures taken with you. That's not bad. I prefer women's company to men's.'

Is it me, or am I listening to more rabbit from the head of a man who's saying what he knows the listener wants to hear? Is it me or is this quote more like it? 'A lady in her nineties lives opposite and she makes meringues like you wouldn't believe. She loves chocolates, so I often buy her a carrier bag of them and go for tea with her.' As Sue Upton said, 'He imagined that he wanted a home and a family, but really didn't want anyone to come that close.'

Chapter 6 Growing Up

'He was hurt as a child, wasn't he?' said Phyllis Diller. 'I can tell. You see, the hurt is the grit in the oyster. It has created the pearl that is his comedy.'

THAT Benny Hill became an entertainer was perhaps pre-ordained. His father, Alfred, had been a circus performer, an acrobat, the 'weakest strong man in the business'. His father's father was a street circus performer. His grandmother's sister was a singer. His father's brother, Leonard, was another circus performer and was killed in a high-wire circus act. It was a heritage that neither Benny nor his brother could deny. By the way, you should hang in here. The Hill family didn't have a great imagination when it came to naming their children, and more often than not opted for the same names again and again. It could get confusing.

Henry, Benny's grandfather, came from a comfortable middle-class background, but was cast out from his family after falling for and running away with a woman the family didn't approve of. Curiously, she too came from a well-to-do family – there were servants and all that caper – but neither family supported the relationship, and once they'd made that decision, things were always going to be hard. Even in the swinging 1960s the assertion that 'All you need is love' was never anything more than a middle-class fantasy. Way back in the 1800s . . . well, you needed a bit more than a cuddle. You

needed a few bob. You needed food on the table. As the family grew and grew, money was a problem. They had to keep moving to avoid the debts. Alfred, Benny's father, told of a time when for his birthday he received the top of his father's boiled egg. That's hard. No money and precious little love. It was the sort of world where you survive by surviving, and if you don't . . . Well, you don't. When he was sixteen, Alfred ran away from home in traditional style to join the circus.

A street-smart man with a keen sense of self, Alfred's world was defined by two contrasting events – the circus and the First World War. Both experiences forged the man, so much so that later in life he developed a kind of split personality. On the one hand there was 'Dad', the playful knockabout circus performer, and on the other there was 'The Captain', his stern, militaristic alter ego. This split personality was OK for story time and play, but there were other times when things got more serious. Alfred had been captured in France and had served as a prisoner of war in Belgium. Now spending any sort of time in Belgium is going to be a life-changing experience, but spending time there as a prisoner of war? It's not going to help, is it?

When he returned from the war, he expected to find life changed, and it had. But had it changed for the better? Alfred's experience was a common one for men returning home after a war. They come back expecting the fanfare treatment, whistles and banners and flags, and maybe there was a bit of that, but 'a land fit for heroes'? It's rarely that. The world has changed, life has changed, relationships have changed. It's dislocating and difficult and why should that be? I've just risked my life for you people. Alfred quickly developed a hatred for authority while still being in its thrall. A couple of business ventures went down the pan, and money had to be earned. He started up a business, a bit of a back-street back-of-the-lorry business selling surgical appliances, including contraceptives. It's a strange thing, but this is pivotal. Fast-forward a few years to Benny in the school playground – all podge with a schoolboy cap and cheeky grin – and the other kids are making fun and laughing. 'Hilly's father sells johnnies.' The other kids are laughing. It's a curious thing this, but they're all laughing at an innuendo gag about sex. They're not actually talking about sex, not mentioning any of the actual bits and pieces, but they're getting a laugh. Anyway.

Alfred and Helen married on 20 June 1920, and eighteen months later their first son Leonard was born. A couple of years later, on 21 January 1924, he was joined by Alfred Hawthorne Hill, aka Alfie, aka Benny, born in a flat above a lamp shop in

Southampton. While Hill's father was the dominant personality, his mother was the love, and it was a mutual infatuation that was going to last a lifetime. 'It's only your father's way,' she'd say in that placatory 'It'll be alright' way that mothers do. Benny's father had a problem with his sons, and it's a problem that's probably more common than we recognize. You meet a woman, you fall in love with her. You want to spend your life with her, you marry her. And then you have children. You both love your children but . . . Does she love them more than she loves you? She's certainly spending more time with them, showering them with more love, more kisses. Before you know it you're jealous of the kids and start to see them not so much as your children but your rivals. It's an animal thing, and probably the reason why so many animals chase their offspring away from the parental nest at what we consider to be an unnaturally early age.

Life at Shirley Infants in the conveniently named Shirley Hill area was much like life at an infants school always is. You play, you get in trouble, you kiss the girls and make them cry. In contrast to his later years, there was never any mistaking which way Benny's rock rolled, and at one stage the school head called Benny's mother in and asked her if she could maybe persuade her son to, how shall we say?, control his excitement. The school was responsible for one other thing, an oft-repeated joke that's always cited as an example of early Hillisms:

A boy comes into the classroom late. A girl is with him.
The teacher: Where have you been?
Boy: Up Shirley Hill.
Teacher (to the girl): And who are you?
Girl: Shirley Hill.

As he grew into his teens, Benny went through a bit of a personality change and grew less confident and more self-conscious. Again, there's nothing particularly radical or significant in this. Adolescence and puberty is a difficult time. Things happen, you change. For Benny, his brother Leonard and his sister Diana, much of the change was related to the increasingly aggressive moods of their father, and as they grew up 'Dad' took more and more of a back seat to 'The Captain'. By and large it was an ordinary prewar life. Holidays in places like Bournemouth and Ryde, a few extra bob, a move

to a bigger house, a scholarship passed and a move to a better school. Another of those spooky events that life sometimes throws up was when he won a scholarship to the local good school. A couple of years earlier his brother Leonard had won a scholarship and there was much celebrating, but when Benny heard in 1935 that he too had won a scholarship he was alone. By himself. He sat in his classroom and was pleased. By himself. Then he ran home to tell his family. But they weren't there. The house was locked, so he sat outside and waited for them to come home and celebrated. By himself. By the time they came home, he'd done with celebrating. He was eleven years old.

The young Hill had developed a love of showing off and performing and seemed a bit of a natural. Impressions came easy, and he took off anyone from Louis Armstrong to Max Miller to Mae West, all with a degree of success. He also showed a smooth proficiency at music, and took up the guitar, the cornet and, most usually, the drums. By the time his age had reached double figures, he was established as the family entertainer and would spend many an afternoon entertaining the family. 'The fool is making his mother laugh again,' his dad would say, while laughing himself.

School didn't offer much of an outlet for the performer boy – the only time he walked on stage there was in a school play version of *Alice in Wonderland*. Benny played a rabbit and said, ''ere, 'ere' a couple of times. Maybe it was a gag.

Young Alfie/Benny's love for the stage came from his grandfather, Harry Hawthorne Hill, better known to the kids as GP. GP had a column in a journal called *The World's Fair*, a magazine for show people. The world was a different place then, and being a critic was a glamorous job. Everyone knew – or wanted to know – GP, and treated him well. It was all very exciting and very romantic to a young boy, and Benny was taken to see small-time names like Horace Goldin, an illusionist, and big stars like Louis Armstrong and Sid Field. Once they went to see a revue called *Naughty Girls of 1937*. It didn't matter what they saw – everything fuelled the fantasies that played themselves out in Benny's bedroom: him the star, his brother Leonard the feed man.

The fourteen-year-old Hill got an audition for a semi-professional outfit called Bobbie's Concert Party, and did a routine doing rubbish jokes and impressions. When this didn't set the skies alight, he put on a dog collar and presented himself as The Minister of Mirth. The gags might have been standard rubbish, but he was already showing a willingness to experiment and a chutzpah that would later set him apart from the pack. There was one other characteristic that had become set. At the end of each show, Alfie/Benny was offered a choice. Half a crown or a taxi-ride home. For Benny it was no choice and, really, he quite enjoyed the walk.

The war came, but that did nothing to dampen his enthusiasms. Days and evenings were spent sitting next to a radio gathering knowledge, information. He would learn the names of all the bands, their leaders and their singers. It was much the same as kids 50 years later would do in front of *Top of the Pops*, but the difference is that while most kids learnt the names and styles and that was about it, young Benny would learn what they sounded like and practise and practise until he would sound exactly like them. Then he would stage a performance in his head.

He supported himself by taking a number of schoolboy jobs, none of which had much significance – well, maybe one did. In 1940, Benny got a job as an assistant milkman. But it was a time when for obvious reasons men were thin on the ground, and he'd soon lost the 'assistant' bit of his title and had his own horse and cart. It must have been fantastic fun for a fifteen-year-old lad, galloping through the streets, just him and Daisy (Daisy was the horse), delivering milk and fruit and veg to all those lonely, left-alone women who wanted to be nice to him because, remember, this was rationing time and young Benny was delivering the food. He had the power.

All the while he was still going to shows, still taking notes, still making plans. By now he was dressed in garish colours, and in the sort of dress that mimicked his great hero, Max Miller. Some of his jokes started to resemble Miller's, but coming out of the mouth of a fifteen-year-old . . . it didn't really work, but it was good experience. In 1941 he made a decision. He'd gone to see a couple of comics called the Smeddle Brothers, not a name that's instantly recognizable now, but the sort of act that made up the bulk of the bills of the old music halls. One day Benny went to see them to ask for advice. He was a young kid and they were proper professionals. So they talked and they talked and the Smeddles . . . Thinking about it, that's not a name built for stardom. If Alfie Hill had to change his name to Benny Hill, what chance the Smeddle Brothers? 'Ladies and gentlemen, tonight at the London Palladium . . . the Smeddle Brothers.' No, it's not going to happen. It wouldn't look good out Caesar's Palace in Luton, never mind Caesar's Palace in Vegas. Still, for the Grand Theatre in Basingstoke it would do just fine. Anyway, the Smeddle Brothers told Benny that he could do it, he had what it took. They persuaded him that he had The Twinkle, and it was all the encouragement a seventeen-year-old lad needed. London was calling.

Chapter 7 Follow That Fun

IT'S a curious thing, but it's often the way. People are remembered as we last saw them, and our last memories of Benny Hill reflect that slightly dodgy, slightly dubious, lecherous telly persona. But back in the 1940s and 1950s he was smart, tough and bright, what we might call today street-smart.

1941 was wartime and the rules were changing by the day. The old certainties became the new uncertainties. Things were fluid and the possibilities were growing. Still, if you were a seventeen-year-old lad from Southampton it still took some bottle to turn round to your parents, tell them you were going to London to try your luck, look them in the eye and admit that you knew no one, had nowhere to stay, no money, no prospects and . . . Listen, I'm just going to give it a go and see what offers. It's just something I've got to do. (Respect to his parents for letting him go. It can't have been easy for them – not for his overbearing father, nor for his mollycoddling mother. It was wartime and he was their baby, but they gave him a few bob and let him go.)

The boy with dreams in his head, Max Miller in his suitcase and a copy of *The Stage* in his hand, he headed off to the West End to see if the streets really were paved with gold, if it was true. In another one of those fortuitous meetings, Alfie/Benny asked a policeman the way to a couple of the theatres listed. The policeman, looking at the young lad and weighing up the situation, recommended that he try his luck out of town

and suggested the Brixton Empress and the Streatham Hill Theatre. It was a smart suggestion. Even in wartime the streets of the West End hold all sorts of perils for a young boy and, apart from anything else, what was the competition going to be like?

There was an act at the Empress, Sid Seymour and the Mad Hatters, that Alfie knew, and that was incentive enough. He was off. The Mad Hatters was an act that . . . well, it was just what it sounded like. A musical experience of people acting crazy with old Sid Seymour trying to keep control. A part as one of the Mad Hatters would have suited young Alfie down to the ground, but Sid didn't have any vacancies. He did though have a brother, Phil, and Phil was an agent. Brother Phil was putting on a show called *Follow That Fun* at the Chelsea Palace, and that's basically what Alfie wanted to do: follow that fun. The Chelsea Palace. It was a place where, many years later, Benny would break box office records, but for now it was the theatre of dreams.

After a few nights sleeping rough on Streatham Common – well, he didn't have much money and what he had he wasn't going to waste on something as decadent as a pillow – and washing in the toilet in Lyons' Corner House, Alfie got his chance. He was ready. He'd been practising during the days on the Common, and if people found anything strange in the sight of a seventeen-year-old boy hanging around the Common talking to himself in the voices of famous film stars and the like, they didn't say so. With a war going on, they had more important things to worry about.

He got the job in *Follow That Fun* – £3 a week – and it proved a great experience, taking him on tour around the country and providing young Alfie with that University of Life education. His job was basically a schlepping job. Filling in, helping out, lending a hand. But it was the start of a life and there was no going back.

Alfie Hawthorne Hill. It was a bit of a mouthful, not the sort of snappy one-liner designed to look good on a poster. Alfie realized this, and had long been billed as Alf Hill, but as his career started to take off . . . it didn't look right, didn't feel right. Alf Hill. It sounded like the name of the local butcher or something. At the suggestion of his brother Leonard, the name Benny was adopted, partly out of a respect for the great comic Jack Benny, though in his book Leonard puts it down to 'the Jewish influence in his chosen profession and the long line of great comedians it had produced'. Benny Hill. It wasn't bad, better than Abie Hill or maybe Moshe Hill, or if Leonard was really serious, maybe Izzy Hillberg.

Alfie became Benny in 1943, and the work flowed. *Follow That Fun* was followed by a spell with a revue based on *Robinson Crusoe*, featuring speciality act Gary Hickson, who tap-danced on his xylophone – yes, he tap-danced on a xylophone and no, don't ask – and in which Benny was 'blacked up' in a sketch called 'The Cannibal King'. 1943. A different world. After *Robinson Crusoe* came *Send Him Victorious*, another touring revue, and after that came . . . something maybe not unexpected, but completely unwanted.

Chapter 8 Gaytime

CRAFTSMAN A. H. Hill, No. 14332308 in the Royal Electrical and Mechanical Engineers. That doesn't sound like much of a stage name, and it wasn't. (Curiously, one of the other privates in his unit was Frankie Howerd, and their paths were going to stay intertwined for the rest of their lives, to the point that they both died on the same weekend, Easter 1992. Ian Carmichael, who he later starred with in the film *Light Up the Sky!* was also in the unit.) Called up in November 1942, Benny didn't see any military action, but was posted to France and Germany. God knows what effect the whole army experience had on his later humour. All those stereotypes to call upon. All that saluting. All that frumpy authority. On a more positive note, there was the Combined Services Entertainment, which provided invaluable experience.

Once Hill signed up with the CSE, things became more bearable. Taken under the wing of another more experienced comic, Harry Segal, Hill became a full-time entertainer. As with many British comics, the war provided not a break from the career but a short cut to the fast lane. It was like being on tour with a revue troupe, albeit a big one. The cast was there, the time to work on scripts and ideas, and, usefully, there was always a captive audience ready and waiting for any relief from the grim tedium of army life. Another useful contact made was a colonel who was sitting in the audience when Hill appeared in a show called *It's All In Fun*. Colonel Richard Stone liked what

BENNY HILL

Paris by Night

he saw – 'I thought Benny was wonderful' – and when he was demobbed and became a showbiz agent, Benny Hill was one of the first people Richard Stone took on.

Five years after he was called up, Benny got his suit and his £50. 1947 was a fine time to be a comic in London. The city was crawling with demobbed talent, fresh out of the army and looking to start where they'd left off. But it was a different story in Civvy Street. In the army they'd had – literally – captive audiences, pleased to see anything and be away from the real business of fighting. Now things were hard-nosed and commercial. Now you had to earn the right. One of the most popular places to find employment was the Windmill Theatre in Windmill Street, home of 'exotic dancers' – strippers – where it was the comic's job to provide the distraction while the next girl prepared herself to get undressed. Some comedians, including Peter Sellers, and Tony Hancock, found work there. Others, including Spike Milligan, Bob Monkhouse and Norman Wisdom, didn't. Benny Hill didn't. The Tottenham Liberal and Radical Club was consolation of a sort, but with that £50 disappearing as quickly as it had come, this was not the time to get precious about 'my art'.

A year of struggle at working men's clubs, telling rubbish jokes, going nowhere and getting increasingly fearful that he'd have to go back to Southampton with his tail between his legs and get a proper job, ended when he found himself playing the Kilburn Empire. Stone was there in his new guise as an agent, and he was with the impresario Hedley Claxton. Together they were putting together a bill for the summer season in Margate. Claxton had booked the cheeky chappie Cockney comic Reg Varney (later to find fame in the ITV sitcom *On the Buses*) to lead and was looking for a support act, a stooge. The competition for the gig was Peter Sellers. Sellers performed a take on George Formby, complete with ukulele and accent. Hill did a calypso number. Hill got the job and the deal was done for £14 a week for the summer season.

The season was called *Gaytime* (no, it didn't mean anything then) and was the usual rude revue nonsense:

> Gaytime, let's have a Gaytime.
> Gaytime, let's have some fun.
> Say so long to trouble and care,
> Let your troubles fly like bubbles,
> Way up in the air.

Hill and Varney gave the summer audiences exactly what they were looking for and went down a storm. The material might have been jaded and corny, but who was listening? They played there for three seasons. Incidentally, it was during the 1950 season of *Gaytime* in Margate that Hill made his first marriage proposal. So nervous that he forced himself to do it from a telephone box, Benny was shot when she turned him down. 'It was a terrible shock. I was so big-headed that I couldn't believe there could be anyone else. That affair really hit me. I had to call the doctor. I was almost suicidal.' He was only 25. Poor dear. We've all been there.

The Varney/Hill partnership was going well. Both were under the watchful wing of Richard Stone and both were getting more popular, better known, more famous. In 1950 they were hired to take over a revue called *Sky High*, which had been playing at the Palladium with Jimmy Edwards in the lead. They took it around the country and generally made a success of the show, but Benny was getting increasingly itchy. A stooge. Is that any way to make a living? How is a man going to become a star playing a stooge? Might the 1950 woman have said 'Yes' if he'd been something more substantial? Benny had had a seven-minute solo spot in the show – a placatory gesture designed to keep the double act together – and generally it went down well. He was a good performer, the material was well suited to the times and the audience, but one night it had misfired spectacularly. They were performing up north in Sunderland, something that was difficult in itself. Variety was a notoriously regional thing. Comics from the north rarely ventured down south – who would understand them? – comics from the south were always given a hard time up north, and the northern Empire circuit was notorious. In Sunderland, what chance did a cheeky Cockerney chappie and a bright-eyed Southampton boy stand? He was slow-handclapped and, within minutes, booed off stage. As Reg Varney recalled, 'Benny tottered in to the dressing room, ashen-faced, and sank into a chair. The door burst open and there was the theatre manager. "Benny Hill?" he shouted. "You're a bloody rotten act." Then he left in a fury. Benny rushed over to the washbasin and was sick into it. He was really ill.' Hill, a fragile ego at the best of times, was shattered, but it strengthened his resolve to leave the act and try his luck on his own.

Chapter 9 Hi There!

HILL persevered with a few more summer seasons at places like Great Yarmouth, and got involved in a bit of panto – he did *Dick Whittington* in Eastbourne – but the writing was on the wall. The world was changing faster than a chorus line's outfits. What was true yesterday, well, who was to say if it'd be true tomorrow? The old rules were changing and the old ways of doing things were changing too. Months and months of slogging around the circuit? You could get more exposure doing fifteen minutes on the radio. There wasn't the intimacy and there wasn't the immediacy – who was to know if they liked your act or not? – and so comics and variety acts started to develop a different approach. But was it good? And, more importantly, did it like you? Radio could take a so-so variety performer and, in less than an hour, turn them into a headlining act. You've got to respect something like that. But with that level of power comes a degree of fear. If radio could take you that high, could it not also take you down? It's more than possible that the name John Gilbert was lurking in more than one or two heads. (If the name John Gilbert evokes the response 'John who?' then the point will have been made. John Gilbert was, famously, the movie star who was killed off by the advent of the Talkies. A huge star in the days of the silent movies, he simply could not make the transition to the new era. Gilbert was a hunk, a real piece of meat. But when they put a microphone under his nose . . . this little squeaky voice popped out.

Shortly after, he decided on a new career in a new bottle.)

Just as all comics of Hill's generation did their time as bit players in *It Ain't Half Hot Mum*, so they also all learnt their trade on the wireless. It was the obvious place for any performer to go after the stage, and you can look at any comic of that era and somewhere there'll be an education at the University of Radio. Unlike other comedians, people like Spike Milligan and Tony Hancock, Benny Hill never became a star of radio. While being valuable experience, it wasn't really his medium. For verbal comics, it was made to measure, but Hill was a much more visual performer. For a comedian in the postwar era the real purpose that it served was to put your name in the frame. You were never going to get on the telly if you hadn't made a bit of a name for yourself on the radio – and so that's what Benny Hill did.

Beginners Please!, Benny's first foray into the world of the wireless, came in 1947 and was basically a talent show, a leg up. The leg up was onto a show called *Variety Band-Box*, a show that didn't do much for Hill but made a star out of Frankie Howerd. After collaborating with Alfred Marks on *Starlight* and with Elsie and Doris Waters (really) on *Petticoat Lane*, Hill did turns in a series of radio variety shows – a spot here, a spot there – but nothing much. He was on *Desert Island Discs* in 1959, but that's not what you'd realistically call a career. In a curious reversal of the way things usually worked, Hill had to wait until he was a star before he fully embraced radio.

Chapter 10 TV Personality of the Year

IN the past, there had always been the feeling that Alfie Hill was still looking for whatever it was that 'Benny Hill' was to become. Alfie had made a bit of a name for himself as a Max Miller soundalike, but when Alfie became Benny he became more successful but hadn't really changed his tactic. When he was Reg Varney's stooge, he was still playing the same game, still being what was maybe his idea of what Benny Hill should be. But when television appeared, that was really when Alfie became Benny. While most of his contemporaries were checking on the map to find out where places like Great Yarmouth were, Benny was plotting and thinking and writing and plotting some more. And as his dissatisfaction grew with being Reg Varney's stooge, Benny increased the tempo.

It was such an obvious irony as to be not really ironic at all. Benny got his first television break as Reg's stooge. Broadcast in 1949, *Here's Mud in Your Eyes* was a revue broadcast live from Alexandra Palace. It was standard revue-type stuff, including a sketch that gave the show its title (the 'mud' was a gooey cocoa concoction), but it was well received and gave Benny hope and ideas. Even though fewer than one in twenty houses had a telly, and the ones that did exist were expensive and not what you'd readily call clear, Benny saw which way the wind was blowing. Later that year, he said, 'The future of entertainment lies with television. That's the star to which I've

hitched my wagon.' Ronnie Waldman, the head of BBC Light Entertainment (and the man who gave Morecambe and Wise their first break and who had rejected Hill in the early days), was targeted and bombarded with scripts and ideas. In 1950, Hill was summoned to see the great man. He'd been working hard and had built up a portfolio of about 40 scripts, so he walked into Waldman's office, put his bag down and said through a mouth full of bravado 'Go on, pick one. Just take one.' Waldman took one, handed it to Benny and sat back as Hill went through the routine. A look turned into a smile and a smile turned into a laugh. 'What are you doing next Thursday?' Ronnie Waldman asked afterwards – and Benny knew.

Waldman knew what he was doing. Never mind that the medium was in its infancy, he knew how it worked. When you go to a theatre, it's a group experience. Even if you go by yourself, you join the audience. You get caught up in the atmosphere, in the feeling. If everyone else is laughing, odds on you'll laugh too, whether you find it funny or not. But television is different. It is, essentially, a private deal, a solo venture. If you laugh it's because you found it funny. Benny made Waldman laugh, and he figured that if he could do that to him, he could probably do it to other people, too.

Hi There! It's a cute name for your first proper TV show, no? It's a name that shows a certain optimism, a certain confidence, and as a gesture Hill started the show with the same sketch that he'd entertained Ronnie Waldman with. It had the same effect, and apart from one critic who moaned about Hill's lack of experience, it was universally well received.

In 1952 Benny ran into his first spot of telly trouble. It was kind of mild compared to the criticism that would dog him in the late 1970s and early 1980s, but it was a shape of things to come. He'd been given a show called *The Centre Show* to host. Again, it was a revue-style show with different acts (including Johnny Dankworth) and Benny gagging away as the host. He was making quite a mark in this nascent medium as a TV personality, but his persona was still largely the cheeky chappie dropping his innocent innuendos and raising his schoolboy titters. Much the same as ever. But this was the BBC of Lord Reith, and *The Centre Show* was filmed at the Nuffield Centre, an army base. The BBC and the army. It wasn't a good combination for this stand-up, stripped-down Max Miller. It didn't take long for the War Office to complain. They

---

Dancing with Rose Hill at The Palace Theatre in Fine Fettle, *1959*

weren't over-impressed with his drag act, Primrose Hill, but the football pools gag . . . Has this man got no shame?

It should go without saying that the football pools gag was maybe the least offensive gag Hill told, but by the same token it's fitting that the War Office should get all upset over what was essentially someone hearing wrong. The gag was this:

'A football pools token was lost in Chelsea last night. Will anyone who finds it, please contact Scotland Yard, telephone Whitehall Home Away, Home Away.'

Oh, calm yourselves down. It wasn't that funny. Actually, it was quite clever. Scotland Yard's phone number was Whitehall 1212, and in football pools terms 1 is a home win and 2 an away win. So. Whitehall Home Away, Home Away. Some brain in the War Office heard the pay-off line as Whitehall homo-way, and as we all know, Whitehall and homosexuality . . . well, it's an outrage. Even thinking about it is an outrage. The net result was that all Hill's future scripts had to be read and checked, but the press coverage . . . Even back in the early 1950s they knew the saying 'Never mind the words, count the column inches.' And Hill had plenty of inches. Oh, be quiet.

It could have been trouble for Hill, but Ronnie Waldman backed him to the hilt and when the War Office got stroppy, Waldman simply withdrew his show from their premises, booked it into the Shepherds Bush Empire and made it bigger and better. What could they say? It was 1953. The war was long gone and people wanted to put all that behind them. The balance of power had shifted.

Benny's next step on the ladder was a programme called *Showcase*. More sophisticated than the revue-style shows, it highlighted his impressionist skills, but the interesting thing was how he was tuning in to what the nearly new medium was doing. Instead of looking back to the days of the comics, Hill was looking at the now, and while that might sound quite a sensible and straightforward way to go, it wasn't what his contemporaries were doing and already started to set him apart from the rest of the field. He started writing sketches that made fun of the other television personalities of the day – chef Philip Harben, DIY king Barry Bucknell, sports commentator Raymond Glendenning, news presenter Cliff Michelmore. These were proper people, but Benny was the first comic to latch on to the fact that when you're on television and you go into someone's living room, you become their friend. People, the viewers, feel that they know the person in the box, and when you make fun of them, it's like having a laugh with a mate in the pub. Right now, Benny Hill was about as cutting-edge as it gets.

Benny as jazz singer Cleo Laine (left) and Henry McGee as husband Johnny Dankworth

In 1954 he did a sketch lampooning the cast of the popular show *What's My Line?*, playing all four panel members (Barbara Kelly, Lady Isobel Barnett, Gilbert Harding and David Nixon). It was a revelation, something that hadn't been seen before, and it established him as Britain's top television comic, the funniest, the most innovative, the yardstick.

Hill was 29 when he did that, and it was a revelation to the young TV audience. The first *Benny Hill Show* on the BBC was broadcast in January 1955 and pulled in 8 million viewers. By February, the *Radio Times* had him on the cover. A star. In 1955 he was voted TV Personality of the Year. And he was pushing back the boundaries, stretching the limits, taking the bus further. Apart from the dead parrot, sorry, the stuffed duck sketch, there were other highlights. The sketch where the BBC commissioning editor tries to persuade a young writer called William Shakespeare to write for him. Thinking about it now, that might sound a bit lame, a bit dull. But this was the 1950s, and no one had done any of this before.

OVERLEAF: Four times the fun. In a technologically revolutionary spoof of current affairs debate programme Free Speech, *1957*

Chapter 11 A Sad Bundle

THERE comes a time in every renaissance man's life when he realizes that he may indeed be a renaissance man but some renaissances work better than others. Hill wasn't a bad comedy actor, but he wasn't film-star material. Maybe he was by now too big a telly star – too recognizable – to make the transition. People saw him and thought 'That's Benny Hill' rather than 'That's Gunner Ted Green' or whatever. But he still aspired, still had dreams. As his brother Leonard notes in his biography *Saucy Boy*, 'As a television comedian in the early 1960s, he considered he had inferior status to his counterparts in the cinema. He recalls an elegant function at which he sat down to dinner next to Richard Todd, the film star. The waiter was most obsequious to the distinguished actor. "Yes Mr Todd. As you wish Mr Todd." To my brother, he babbled as he filled his plate, "Ere y'are, Ben. Git this lot dahn yer an' you'll be as fat as a pig."'

Benny Hill's film career was not a sparkling success – you can count the films he made on the fingers of one hand – and none made the critics line up outside his house, ready to offer their congratulations. Doesn't matter. Three of those films were very good films in their own terms. *Those Magnificent Men in Their Flying Machines* was a classic slapstick comedy, *Chitty Chitty Bang Bang* was a truly scrumptious children's yarn, while *The Italian Job* was a genuine landmark movie. It's not a bad CV.

1955. Benny Hill was a star. He had his own television show, more viewers than

Ealing Studios Present a Michael Balcon Productio

BENNY HILL
in
WHO DONE IT? (

Also starring
Belinda Lee   David Kossof   Garry M

anyone else, and a presence. This was Benny's time, and when you're 30 you've got enough energy for more than one project at a time. He signed up to appear in the Folies Bergère show, *Paris By Night*, at the Prince of Wales Theatre (where he was supported by Tommy Cooper) and was a huge success. 'When it was announced that we were featuring Benny, we had the biggest advance orders ever,' said Lord Delfont. 'He was a tremendous draw. The theatre was booked for eighteen months solid.' It was classic music hall stage humour – coarse, rude and laced with sexual innuendo. Visual.

Beautiful models surrounded by not so beautiful men. Trousers that fell down. Maybe a banana-skin gag.

Benny was putting in two performances a night when he started work on his first feature film. Directed by Basil Dearden and scripted by Ealing legend TEB Clarke, *Who Done It?* was what we'd call now a 'star vehicle': a film written specially for Hill, and designed to appeal to his growing number of telly fans. In 1954, Clarke followed Hill around the country, picking up tips, soaking it all in. He wanted to see how Benny worked, how he reached people. It just shows you. You can do too much research. Even though Ealing's best days were behind it, you'd have thought with a team like that to back you . . . But no, it wasn't a great success. Ealing Studios decided not to premiere the film in London. 'I found it a sad bundle,' wrote Dilys Powell in the *Sunday Times*. 'The situations and stock ingredients made it corny,' said *Variety*. Apparently Benny proposed to co-star Belinda Lee while they were making the film. She also said no.

Meanwhile, back in the more comfortable world of television . . . Benny had hooked up with co-writer Dave Freeman and the *Benny Hill Shows* were going from strength to strength. Hill wrote, Freeman laughed. Freeman wrote, Hill laughed. Things were going well. The *Radio Times* decided to cast him in a cartoon, calling him 'Britain's Brightest Boy'.

Things were also going well for television. It was getting bigger, more important. The sets were coming down in price and becoming more accessible. To Benny and Dave, this was just what they wanted – more material. Any TV shows that became successful, any personalities who became well-known, this was just more of the raw material they needed. *Juke Box Jury*, *Dixon of Dock Green*, naturalists Armand and Michaela Denis, Hans and Lotte Hass . . . shows and personalities that mean nothing now (well, not unless you've got a bus pass in your bag), but that were household names in those days.

Benny's ability to mimic – the result of all those years of practice, going back to his youth in Southampton, the grim days sleeping rough on Streatham Common – was invaluable and, aligned with the technical advances being made . . . well, man and medium were made for each other. The BBC, for all its stuffy reactionary ways, recognized the talent it had on its hands. In 1956 Hill was on £350 a show. Fantastic money. But not as fantastic as the £650 he got in 1957. A memo from Tom Sloan, who had taken over from Ronnie Waldman as head of Light Entertainment, let slip that the BBC would have paid £1,000 if it had to. Dave said to anyone who would listen that 'He could last for thirty years if he doesn't do too much of it.'

It was around this time that Ronnie Waldman received that internal BBC memo ('Subject: *The Benny Hill Show*, Saturday 1 February 1958. This, I thought, was in places brilliant. At the same time I am always worried that Hill will say or do something unacceptable.') Pick a contemporary comic, any contemporary comic. A later sketch about the pop show *Juke Box Jury* played essentially the same game as the *What's My Line?* sketch, but this time Benny wanted all four characters (again, all played by him) to appear on the screen at the same time, to interact. It's a different thing, but it's like when the Beatles first said to George Martin, 'Yeah, that sounds good. But what does it sound like backwards?' It was a leap of imagination, a leap of technical expertise, a leap of faith.

Britain's Brightest Boy was smart enough to realize that if he wasn't careful he'd get pigeonholed as someone who did sketches about television personalities. Maybe it was time to create a few characters. And so it was that in 1957, a juddering idiot threw up a salute. Fred Scuttle – a character who was to become intertwined with Hill to the extent that sometimes it was difficult to see the join – was born.

Things were going so well that Benny couldn't believe that the film world would escape his grasp for long. But … 'Of all the lying, perverse, dangerous tributes to the merry romps of our brave lads in that difference of opinion 20 years ago, *Light Up the Sky* is the most appalling,' wrote the critic of the *Tribune*. The review went on, but you probably get the idea. Directed by Lewis Gilbert in 1960 and starring Ian Carmichael and Tommy Steele, *Light Up the Sky* was the story of a music hall double act (Hill and Steele) who are called up. Hill had some fun writing the corny stage-show sequences, nicking gags from his own past, and worked quite well with Steele, but it wasn't where he wanted to be.

Chapter 12 'Crumpet, of Course'

WHILE the would-be film career was floundering, Hill found consolation in two unlikely places: advertising and radio.

Benny and Dave were employed by Schweppes to make a series of ads that netted a small fortune – not that he was overly impressed by the industry. 'The advertising business is self-indulgent, so many unnecessary conferences, such long lunches. For five years I made more cash from the commercials than from anything else. I got a fantastic amount of money. The contract involved me in two weeks' work a year, from which I received enough to live in luxury for the rest of the year without doing a stroke. Ridiculous. People in this business are hopelessly and idiotically overpaid.' Still, it was a useful practice ground. There was money to experiment and play, to try out things they hadn't tried. Benny invented a new bunch of characters. Dave played with the technique of speeding up film that was to become such a trademark. There was kudos too. An ad he made in 1961, selling tomato juice, won first prize at the Cannes International Festival of Commercials. Recognition. It was nice.

So television continued to grow and Hill continued to grow with it. But there was a feeling within the BBC that those revue-type shows had had their day. Situation comedies, that was the way forward. Well, sitcoms were cheaper and easier to produce. You could develop the characters, take them somewhere. Benny was reluctant to get involved with this. Whatever its strengths, whatever its faults, *The Benny Hill Show* had always been a bit of an event. But a sitcom? That's just a sitcom. Nice and clever and good and all that stuff, but not special.

By now the BBC and Benny Hill were two powerful bodies, and when bodies collide . . . they came to a compromise. Hill would make one-off sitcoms. Short dramas. Self-contained stories with a beginning, a middle and an end. It would be acting more than simply being a comic. It would stretch him and make up for the film failures. It might even make a few film producers sit up and take notice. Benny made nineteen short drama sitcoms, the first six written by him and Dave, the rest by Dave alone. Popular enough, they weren't that popular. Maybe it was the old story of the public not being ready to accept someone they were familiar with in a different role. Maybe the idea of a half-hour comedy drama was still a bit too complex. Whatever, it didn't really happen, and Benny went off and did the only thing that a man in that situation can do: he went off and played Bottom in *A Midsummer Night's Dream*.

In 1964 he tried to kick-start the film career and took a part in *Those Magnificent Men in Their Flying Machines*, a farce intended to recapture the days of old when stars were silent and dialogue a futuristic notion. Which was perfect for Benny but like others in the film, his part was little more than a high-profile cameo.

Also in 1964, Hill got his only star-billed radio show. *Benny Hill Time* capitalized on his success on BBC television and gave him a nice break from the hard work of the situation comedy dramas and the nonsense of the film world. Fred Scuttle was still a new character and the gags were fresh. His wordplays were still clever and didn't rely so much on dubious double entendres for effect. Well, on the radio there was no chance of doing that sideways leer to the camera to milk the laugh. It's ironic in a sense, but it was during this period that Benny Hill, the comedian, was possibly at his peak. Ironic because Benny Hill is a visual comic. Ironic because radio was the medium he cared least about.

He wrote a screenplay, *I Love You, I Love You, I Love You*, which attracted the attention of John Boorman but didn't get further than the chat stage. The film career stalled again. Ego aside, it didn't really matter that film didn't want him. None of his contemporaries had success on the big screen, nor were they going to. Morecambe and Wise were also big stars, big too in America, with a regular slot on the *Ed Sullivan Show*, yet their big bid for movie glory ended with a bunch of reviews you couldn't

Benny centre, to the left of Michael Caine, in a rare press photo to advertise The Italian Job, 1969

make up. Made in 1963 for Rank, *The Intelligence Men* was a disaster. 'In *The Intelligence Men* we have to watch the ruination of two excellent comics in an embarrassingly unfunny skit,' said the *Sunday Express*, which just about summed up the tone. Charlie Drake, Tony Hancock, Cannon and Ball . . . big screen and little rarely seem to mix, the cross-over hardly ever happens. What cracks us up in our living rooms seems to leave us ice-cold in the cinema.

What the hell. Benny got over the disappointments of *Those Magnificent Men* and the aborted scripts resulting from the BBC asking him to make another television series. It might not have pushed the boundaries or stretched his talents, but it was what he did best. The BBC put it forward for the Golden Rose of Montreux, and in 1966 he was voted BBC Television Personality of the Year. That same year, he finished *Benny Hill Time*, the last radio series he was to make for the BBC. There was also a downside to this period. His long-time collaborator Dave Freeman left to strike out on his own.

In 1968, he got another bite of the cherry. Cubby Broccoli, the man behind the Bond films, had got hold of another Ian Fleming book and was preparing to turn it into *Chitty Chitty Bang Bang*, starring Dick Van Dyke. Broccoli had Hill in mind for the part of Caractacus Potts, a mad German inventor, and asked Hill to rewrite the part to make it funnier. 'When we were introduced I felt a little in awe of Dick Van Dyke. I had never met him before and felt rather uneasy about my role of supporting actor. I had been Top Banana in my own show, now Dick was Top Banana and I had to keep a lower profile.' It's understandable. For as long as he could remember Benny was in sole command, and for such an unreconstructed control freak, it must have been difficult to take the part of a bit player in such a big production. But Dick was 'an awfully nice man. And he was so professional, so highly disciplined in his work.'

Sweetly, Benny remarked later that 'when I made a television commercial in which I did a funny piece made up as a dog with floppy ears and a red nose, Dick was very complimentary and made sure I knew he had seen it and had liked it.'

Chitty Chitty Bang Bang was a big success, though whether it made much difference to Benny's career is debatable. It cemented Dick Van Dyke's name but that was about it. Like Sally Ann Howes', who played the truly scrumptious Truly Scrumptious, Benny's gain was strictly short-term. But he was such a big star that film producers continued to knock on his door, figuring that he could open the way to a different audience. In 1968 Troy Kennedy Martin, a respected television scriptwriter who was known mainly for the BBC cop series *Z Cars*, sent him a script for a heist caper called *The Italian Job*. The part he was offered was Professor Peach, another eccentric inventor type whose job it was to control the traffic patterns of Turin while the gang made their getaway. Hill made one demand to change the script, and it was a fantastically Hillesque request. Originally the character was written as being mad about model trains – he was an eccentric, remember? – and in the script it was written that in payment for his role in the job, Peach was to receive a giant train set. For Benny this was out of the question.

'I couldn't imagine anyone going on a bullion raid, risking their neck for a train set. It was bizarre.' And so what did Benny suggest would be a suitable temptation? 'Crumpet, of course.' Of course. Benny got the green light and rewrote the part to suit himself. Not a woman. Women. Two women. Fat women. Comedy women.

Starring Noël Coward and Michael Caine (and, actor/comedian Henry McGee in a bit part), *The Italian Job* was a huge success, and is still considered a key film. However, for Benny it proved to be a bit of a swansong. The irony is that it was both the best film he was involved in and the most successful, but as far as he was concerned it signalled the end of his celluloid career. Benny decided to give his character some character, and played Peach as a deaf Yorkshireman. Why? Only he knows. Not so surprisingly, the producers doubted that this kind of characterization would have much in the way of international appeal, and made him redub his lines in standard American digestible English. 'That took the edge off the character, and most of the humour went down the plughole. My disappointment led me to resolve that in future I would keep control of my own work.'

That 'keep control of my own work' line said it all, and drew the line under his film career. It also put paid to his time at the BBC.

Chapter 13 A Phenomenon

FOR all his innovation and all his trailblazing televisual trickery, Benny Hill will forever be remembered for his years at Thames TV, and to this day he remains the consummate ITV comedian. Thames had been set up in 1968 and quickly established itself as the more . . . how shall we say? . . . populist arm of television. It was, in crude terms, the working-class side that counterbalanced the more refined BBC.

That Hill went to Thames at all was something of a surprise. He'd been riding high at the BBC, and in 1968 he'd had the big Boxing Day prime-time special. The relationship looked to be flourishing. For Thames it was a coup, showing their power in the marketplace and their ability to compete with the BBC on equal terms. For Hill, it was a good move too. At the BBC he'd been a star, one of the biggest, but at Thames he was *the* star. And that's a vital difference. The arguments that were used to tempt him to cross the line were strangely similar to those that Thames used to tempt Morecambe and Wise a decade later. Apart from the buckets of extra cash – the BBC always took the very BBC attitude that you should be grateful to work for them – Thames offered him colour, the chance to direct his own films, and a greater scope to work in film. One of the key factors in his leaving the BBC was that they decided not to repeat his 1969 series. He thought they were going to. It was his understanding, his belief, that they were going to, and their decision not to . . . Well, to Benny it represented yet another example of things being done without his say-so, things over which he had no control. Clearly, it was time to get out.

Hill was already a little disillusioned with life at the BBC. In particular, three of the directors he'd worked so closely with – Duncan Wood, John Street and Kenneth Carter – were no longer on the team, and this was a matter of paramount importance. More than any other performer Hill was a team man. He liked to have the same people around him all the time. It made him feel secure. He didn't have to explain himself, didn't have to pretend to be something he wasn't. Wherever you look through Hill's career, he's surrounded by his own people. You don't need deep psychological insight to see the importance of a tight team and secure surroundings to a man who has no family, no children, precious few friends and little of what you might call a social life. How many times do you hear people say things like 'My work is my life'? Well, Hill was in a position to make that sentiment come absolutely true.

Typically, when he packed his bags for the BBC he didn't go alone. Henry McGee, Bob Todd, Jenny Lee-Wright and Jack Wright – people who'd all worked with Hill on his last three BBC specials – also packed their bags. While they all, no doubt, felt a sense of personal loyalty, it's not hard to see why they took Benny's shilling. McGee and Todd were consummate comedians in their own right – McGee the straight man, Todd the comic stooge – and while it's likely that they'd have got work elsewhere, the Hill show was a regular gig, a job they'd worked for and made their own. Given the chance of carrying on, of course they were going to take it. Jenny Lee-Wright and Jack Wright, what were they going to do without their employer? Little Jack Wright was by now so typecast as Hill's bald plaything that he had no choice. What was he going to do? Hope that Eric Morecambe fancied running around patting him on the head?

Regardless of what history makes of Benny Hill and his comedy, there can be no doubt that during his time at Thames he moved from being merely a very successful comedian to something much more significant: he became a cultural phenomenon. Immediately, he hit a home run. Though the show was largely the same old thing – a vicar with his flies undone, sexy nurses in frilly underwear – the punters loved it. Curiously, though, as was the case throughout his career, the critics lined up to knock the show (I'm sure we could get a gag in here about knockers) and out came all the usual criticisms. It was banal, rude, lowest common denominator nonsense. But as the critics took their positions, so the viewers took theirs – in front of the telly.

The familiar Benny Hill Show *lineup. L-R: Henry McGee, Hill, Jackie Wright*

Philip Jones, the head of Light Entertainment at Thames, had signed Hill for four one-hour specials, and each show he did got better ratings than the last one. Given that they started off at a peak, it's little wonder that Thames were pleased. The more the viewers tuned in, the happier Thames became, and the happier Thames became the more willing Philip Jones was to let Hill do whatever he pleased. And so the bikinis shrank, the camera angles lingered that extra second or two, and the leers got that little bit leerier. Jenny Lee-Wright found her parts getting bigger. As it were. And the further this went, the more the British public tuned in.

Benny was named ITV Personality of the Year in 1969. His ratings topped the 20 million barrier. A compilation of his four specials was put together and entered for the Montreux Festival. All very impressive, but the most impressive statistic is this: in 1969, *The Benny Hill Show* got higher ratings than the Apollo moonshot. It's an astounding thought, and quite what it tells us I'm not sure. More people wanted to watch Benny Hill leer at Jenny Lee-Wright's half-concealed breasts than watch Neil Armstrong take that first step on the moon. More people wanted to watch Benny Hill slap Jackie Wright's head than see that one giant leap for mankind. Is that not an astounding thought? What on earth does it tell us about evolution?

The Montreux Festival bid – part of Thames's strategy for selling Hill to a worldwide audience – featured one of his famed multi-screen sketches, a skit on the Eurovision Song Contest. These were the days of Eurovision's pomp and, like Hill himself, it was part of the national fabric. To combine the two was a master stroke. In it he played host Katie Boyle (Katie Boiled) and all six entrants.

Back at Thames HQ, the general feeling was that Hill would walk it, and maybe he did. But a Czech film, *Six Fugitives*, walked quicker and got the award. A completely silent film, this maybe was the moment that saw Hill turn away from inventive comedy and move towards the silent slapstick that he grew up loving. After all, if *The Benny Hill Show* was too sophisticated for the burghers of Montreux, there was only one way for it to go.

The ratings for *The Benny Hill Show* continued to rise and, as they rose, Hill's power within the Thames organization grew. Despite the growing chorus of criticism, Hill persisted with the skimpy costumes and the cleavage gags, and even created a character, Mervyn Cruddy, to bait those puritans who dared find fault. The simple truth was that Hill's popularity had made him too powerful to criticize.

That year, 1971, proved quite a high water mark for Hill. His 1971 season won a BAFTA, and he won an award for the Funniest Person on Television. At the British Screen and Television Awards he won three awards, including Best Light Entertainment Programme and Best Scriptwriter. 1971 also provided Benny with another highlight.

> I said you'll have it pasteurized cos pasteurized is best,
> She said 'Ernie I'll be happy if it comes up to my chest.'
> That tickled old Ernie
> And he drove the fastest milkcart in the West.

'Ernie' was a fantastic song. It was the era of rubbish novelty songs, and Christmas was when they all came out of the woodwork. But 'Ernie' was a fantastic song. Inspired by his days as a milkman in Southampton and supported by a custom-made film (the first pop video?), it was Hill at his peak. Knowing innuendo sat happily next to lewd leer and nothing at all dodgy was said. Well, not unless you had the ears to hear it.

'The song was partly autobiographical. When I say "He galloped into Market Street, his badge upon his chest," that was me. As I had a country round, they always gave me the most spirited horse, so when I returned I let them know I was coming, over Station Hill, round into Leigh Road and swinging into Market Street, we galloped as fast as we could. I imagined I was driving the stagecoach into Dodge City, hoofs drumming, bottles rattling and every living thing flying out of our way.'

'Ernie' stayed at number one for five weeks.

Chapter 14 A Marriage Made in Heaven

BENNY Hill first saw Dennis Kirkland in 1966. Hill was rehearsing a sketch where he was a ballet dancer, fat and ungainly, and . . . well, you can guess how the sketch progressed. As Hill was jumping around, pirouetting and falling over, Kirkland sat in the corner and burst out laughing. 'Book him. Sign him up!' said Benny. 'He's a good audience. We must have him.' Kirkland proved to be an integral part of the Hill phenomenon, as much a part as McGee, Wright and any number of Hill's Angels, and worked in some capacity on every show that Hill made for ITV.

He made the final transition to (almost) equal when he became director in 1978 (Hill referred to him as his 'writer's labourer'), and by then Kirkland knew Benny's ways and foibles better than anyone. Working with Benny was often a tense and fraught time. It's the way. Possibly the two worst kinds of people to work for are control freaks and comic geniuses. Remember, Hill was such a control freak that he refused to sanction an official fan club on the grounds that although it would have something to do with his life, it would be out of his own hands. Remember that this was a man whose shows pulled in 20 million viewers, a man who had an unprecedented degree of power at Thames TV. Can you imagine how many corporate suits queued up to tell him what a comic genius he was? Control freaks and comic geniuses. When you combine the two . . . it's a combustible concoction.

As Sue Upton said, 'My relationship with Benny changes slightly when we're working. It's suddenly professional again. He's employing me. I feel nervous, on my

toes, just one of the girls. Of course, I realize that the show claims one hundred per cent of his thought, his time and his effort. And, if he gives me a word of praise, it makes my week. Then, once the show is finished, we slip back into our casual friendship again.' Nicholas Parsons, the pre-McGee suave straight man, said, 'I enjoyed working with Benny. He was always so disciplined, friendly and helpful. It's true that he was a trifle tense at the final recording, but that was to be expected. The man was carrying a tremendous weight of responsibility. The show had to be right. And Benny was at the centre of it, with complicated songs, quick changes, different characters. He knew all our livelihoods were at stake. One duff show, one duff sketch even, and the critics would pounce. No wonder he was tense.'

Kirkland, who cut his television teeth on *The Sooty Show* and was Tommy Cooper's producer and confidant, understood all this. Working with the unpredictable was second nature to him – can you imagine what a day in the studio with Tommy Cooper was like? – but, more importantly, Kirkland was a man of comedy. He was the perfect foil for Hill. Where some of Hill's previous producers might have chickened out of some of his more risqué items, that wasn't Kirkland's style. 'When you have a world-beater like Benny, you let him run. You don't stand on his toes. I give him as much room as I can. Let him follow his fantasy. I never say, "No, we can't do that. We can't afford that." Or, "You're crazy. It's just not possible." Let him dream, let him play. Improvise, juggle with it then, when he has perfected the crazy comedy notion, think about ways of bringing it to the screen. If we do this, it might work. It might be practicable. If we do it this way, it might be cheap enough to put on. Never cut him down. Never stifle his imagination.' Kirkland never did stifle Hill's imagination and, more often than not, the results were plenty cheap.

It helped that the two men were as one on matters of comedy. Slapstick has got itself a bit of a reputation as being the humour of the stupid, but it's not that simple. What would you call, for example, Spike Milligan's work? Surreal or slapstick? Most people would label it 'surreal', but that's only so that they can justify it intellectually. In truth, take away Milligan's maniacal grin and replace it with Benny Hill's idiot leer, and what's the difference? Both relied on visual gags, both fell down a lot, and both used semi-clad women to get cheap, instant laughs. It's a thin line, no? Both Hill and Kirkland were infatuated with the 'visual', a style of comedy that hybridized the slapstick tradition of the silent age and the knockabout blue humour of the music hall. A little bit Charlie Chaplin, a little bit Max Miller. Kirkland was more into the slapstick, Hill more into the Blue Max, but that's splitting hairs. It was a marriage made.

'To make people laugh is a privilege. It's the sound of all sounds, it's the sound of life. "A joke's not funny till it's been laughed at." Eric Morecambe said that. Or was it Benny? Doesn't matter. They probably got it from someone else.'
Dennis Kirkland

It was under Kirkland's direction that the famous chase sequences that closed the show found full expression, and what had previously been little more than homages to the silent comedy kings became films in their own right, often clocking in at over five minutes' length. Kirkland used a technique called undercranking to achieve that Chaplinesque quality. Films were shot at 18 frames per second but run at 24 frames per second, and looked jerky and cranky, just like those films of old. Throw in a handful of semi-clad lovelies, add a little bit of Boots Randolph's 'Yakety Sax' and you've got the biggest-selling comedy show in the world.

Morecambe and Wise, Tommy Cooper, The Ronnies, Dick Emery . . . pick your own comic icon, but great as they were, all these shows had basically one groove that they worked in. There were times during the mid-1970s when you'd know about 70 per cent of *The Morecambe and Wise Show* without even watching it. There'd be a statue on the stage, you'd know its mouth would move, and it would make some reference to Luton Town FC. It didn't take anything away from anyone's enjoyment of the thing – on the contrary, it reinforced it. It made you feel like you were in a club. It was the same with *The Benny Hill Show*. During the mid-1970s, that period when he went from merely huge to enormous, his shows gradually became more and more predictable. The sketches. The characters. The gags. There was an increasing reliance on fewer things. Slapping Jackie Wright's head. The Fred Scuttle character. The clever wordplays that put naughty words in innocent surrounds. The still lewd, still saucy – pre-explicit – Max Millerisms. Hill hit a rich vein of comedy that sat somewhere between that music hall ethos, Chaplin, and the Don't Lose Your Trousers Vicar-type farces of Ray Cooney, and the public lapped it up. Words like 'knickers' – why, we Brits just can't get enough.

U TURN

ME ON

RURAL DISTRICT COUNCIL

But it wasn't all jollity and light. Well, it never was going to be, was it? As successful as Hill got, so his real life went more and more the other way. His dietary habits ran wildly out of control and his weight fluctuated. He got depressed about that and so found refuge the classic way. He ate more food. And when he didn't eat food, he ate appetite-suppressing amphetamines. In 1976, the serious signs that his body was having trouble keeping up appeared when he was diagnosed with kidney failure and had to have one kidney removed.

There was much worse to come in 1976. It was the year that his mother died. The Captain had passed away in 1972 and, sad as that was, it didn't cut deep. She bequeathed her son the family home in Southampton on condition that he never sold it. And despite an intrusive press that went out of its way to portray Benny as some kind of Norman Bates character, he never did.

Chapter 15 Hitting Gold

THEY might not immediately seem like soul brothers, but Benny Hill and Woody Allen have a surprising amount in common. The obvious example is in their attitudes to women. Both have made careers out of chasing young women (on screen), and both have seen those careers flounder on what we might call an over-enthusiastic reliance on that tactic. Both have been pilloried by a public who have maybe been confused by their personas, mistaking the screen version for the real thing. Both are, professionally, lone wolves, creators who see, feel and live the end-product. Both know the value of surrounding yourself with a loyal team who will protect you and create the space for you to practise your art. Not only has Allen always had a core of Allen-friendly actors, from Tony Roberts and Diane Keaton in the early days through to Dianne Wiest and Sidney Lumet in later films, but the production team has remained pretty stable. Cinematographer Gordon Willis. Casting by Juliet Taylor. Edited by Susan E. Morse. Produced by Charles H. Joffe and Jack Rollins. It was the same for Benny Hill.

At the same time as being controlling, Benny Hill was reliant on the team. Watching his shows it's easy to see; Henry McGee, stooge Jack Wright, comedian Bob Todd, Hill's Angels Sue Upton and Jenny Lee-Wright. But the team behind Benny counted as much as those in front of the camera. Producer Dennis Kirkland. Philip Jones, head of Light Entertainment at Thames. His agent Richard Stone. Don Taffner, head of marketing at Thames.

Taffner came on board in 1968, when Thames TV first started. An old school showbiz agent from Brooklyn, it was his job to try and sell Thames's programmes abroad. That was his job. Selling Benny Hill to the States was his mission. But it wasn't easy. The format was all wrong for the format-obsessed American programmers – an hour show? Who wants to watch an hour show? And while Benny wasn't some parochial end-of-the pier British no-name, he still wasn't big enough to persuade the States to take a shot.

A combination of Taffner's shrewd dealing, innovative programming ideas and a touch of luck turned the negative into a positive. A friend of a friend was the manager at a struggling station in Philadelphia, WTAF. Ratings were down and the advertisers were getting twitchy. Something had to be done if the trend was to be reversed – but who'd have guessed that that something would be a podgy, ribald English comic? Together, station manager Ron Gold and Taffner cooked up the idea of re-editing Hill's shows into handy bite-sized chunks. Thirty minutes – well, twenty once the adverts had been taken into account – of fast-cut Hill. No bumbling Fred Scuttle monologues. No fancy wordplays. No cumbersome set-ups. No British reference points. Just thirty minutes of the visual, which essentially was rude slapstick. John Street, who had once been Benny's director at the BBC but was now retired, was the man put in charge of the editing.

WTAF decided to roll the dice. Ron Gold, the station manager at WTAF, decided to strip the show – show it at the same time every day of the week, starting 8 January 1979. As a strategy, it was unheard of. Saturation scheduling. There would be no time to build the publicity machine, no time to market the show, to make sure people knew who Hill was. Mad or desperate, Gold made his play. Then a curious thing happened. People started watching. The reviews the show got in the local press were uniformly friendly. Philadelphia liked Benny Hill. And that was only the beginning. Once Philadelphia bit, other stations began to take notice, and one by one local stations across America took up an option on the Hill show.

Gold and Taffner couldn't have planned it better if they'd tried. There'd been no national campaign, none of the major networks were involved, so there'd been no serious hype. Benny Hill crept across America, fuelled by word of mouth and local knowledge. It wasn't a corporate thing, it was the people's thing, and that made it all

the better, all the more popular.

When anything becomes that popular, a strange thing happens. People start to try to be associated with it, they like to be seen with it or seen to be talking about it. And so it was – the phenomenon that was *The Benny Hill Show* in America. There was all the usual stuff, like conventions, but there was something extra. Car stickers, T-shirts, badges. People held Benny Hill parties. TV stations had Benny Hill weekends. A proper phenomenon. In 1980 and 1981, the show was nominated for the Emmys. When Benny and Dennis Kirkland visited the States, Clint Eastwood sent a message of good luck, Jack Lemmon paid a visit, Burt Reynolds threw a party. Hugh Hefner opened his doors (a dangerous ploy, you'd have thought). The *Daily Mail* wrote: 'Bruce Forsyth tried to and couldn't, Morecambe & Wise wanted to but didn't, Benny Hill, without even trying, has succeeded. He is the first English comic to appear coast to coast in America in his own series.' It's all true, but maybe the most interesting point is that line about 'without even trying'. Hill's American success happened if not despite him, then certainly without him. There were no exhausting tours, no slogging it out on the self-promotion trail. Hill stayed at home making his shows and watching his multiple televisions, and America fell like a row of dominoes.

Part of the reason was that American television was, and still is, astoundingly prudish. For all the upfront sex in its film industry, precious little in the way of flesh is allowed on American telly. It's something to do with corrupting the morals of a nation. If you want to appear on TV and tell gullible people that you're an emissary of The Lord, and if they give you the contents of their credit cards you'll put in a Good Word, while all the time you're lying through your teeth about your life and wife and humping your neighbours' favourite Labrador . . . that, apparently, is OK. Flash a nipple, though, and . . . the very fabric of society is likely to fall apart. Looking back now, it's easy to see. Benny Hill – lewd, crude, nudge-nudge Benny Hill – was always going to appeal to a nation with more sexual hang-ups than a wardrobe has hangers. Hill's schoolboy snigger, that seaside postcard saucy smut, was a winner because we all like looking at breasts and legs and bottoms and all that spectacular flesh, but if we have to deal with it in an adult way . . . Shut that door, draw those curtains. It's perhaps telling that the only note of dissent from the American press came in the urbane, sophisticated *Village Voice*, which talked of Hill's 'pornographic grubbiness'.

Chapter 16 Hello Boys

'I'm not against naked women. Not as often as I'd like to be.'
Benny Hill

TOP of the Pops had pioneered the idea of the sexy dancer with its dance troupe Pan's People – and how many teenage boys used to sit and watch *Top of the Pops* working out how many fast songs there'd been and how many slow songs, and hoping that they were saving back a fast song for the Pan's People number, because in the slow songs they wore all that long, floaty rubbish – you couldn't see anything. The fast songs were much better. In the fast songs they needed to be that much freer, so naturally they needed to be unimpeded by clothing.

As the 1970s progressed, Pan's People turned into Legs & Co., a dance troupe that used essentially the same dancers but squeezed them into smaller clothes. As the walls were coming down the boundaries were being pushed out, and as the boundaries were pushed . . . the cleavages got deeper. These progressive versions of Pan's People might have got up the noses of Mary Whitehouse and those fine folk at the National Viewers and Listeners Association (never a bad thing), and they might have delighted schoolboys of all ages, but really they were little more than increasingly risqué versions of the same thing. They might have titillated, but they didn't challenge, they didn't

really offend. They did what they were expected to do.

It took a maverick to take the next step. For all his unpredictability, Kenny Everett could always be relied on to do one thing: upset people. Whatever anyone else was doing, Everett had to take it further, and as *Top of the Pops* pressed on with their quaint dancers, Everett took the ball and kicked it as far as he could. Hot Gossip blew the opposition out of the water. A cross-gender, cross-racial dance troupe who boasted maybe one costume between them, they were properly outrageous. Raunchy and sexually aggressive, they weren't fey and coy like past troupes. Somehow you got the impression that you weren't looking at them, they were looking at you. Hot Gossip took the form as far as it would go. The way those big black boys picked up those featherlite white girls . . . Really, to have been any more explicit you'd have needed a licence.

Using women as part of the set design wasn't new. Listen, where would Wilson and Keppel have been without Betty? Comic icons since time began had exploited women. Morecambe and Wise weren't adverse to the odd bit of semi-clad. Hill himself had been using women since his days at the BBC. But it was in the mid-1980s that things came to a head. In fairness, what choice did Hill have? He'd made a name for himself using girls. His show had a reputation for showing acres of skin, for being the place to go for a bit of light titillation. What could he do? Suddenly everyone was playing the same game and doing it better than him. Programme one shows a thigh. Programme two shows something a bit higher. What can programme three show?

Hill's Angels were officially launched on 6 February 1980. Aided by Dennis Kirkland, one of the best and most successful light entertainment producers Britain has ever had, Benny decided that Everett had made his girls look a little bit tame. He decided the time was ripe to push the boat out, and really he was right. It was the year after *The Benny Hill Show* started in America, and by 1980 his stock had never been higher. He was a huge star, not just in England, not just in Australia but worldwide. He was earning huge amounts for Thames and, really, if he'd come up with an idea involving young goats, Thames would have been pushed to say no.

But even here, Hill ran into problems. It wasn't simply the question of which troupe showed more flesh – comparing Hill's Angels and Hot Gossip you'd have been pushed to say who was more explicit – it was a question of context. Hot Gossip were a dance troupe. They would dance to a song and that would be that. Nothing really was changed from the days of Flick Colby and her Pan's People. They were there as much for the little girls to aspire to as for the older men to lech at. You knew that girls watched *Top of the Pops* and dreamt of being in Pan's People. You knew that girls watched Kenny Everett and dreamt of being in Hot Gossip. It was so glamorous, so exotic. Both troupes were, for all their titillation value, presented as being primarily concerned with dance. They were dancers. That's what they were there for. If you found them sexy or titillating, all well and good.

From the off, there was something different about Hill's Angels. You got the feeling that while all that was true about Hot Gossip and the rest, the opposite was true of Hill's Angels. Their primary function was to titillate. If they could dance as well, all well and good. It was very difficult to imagine a young girl sitting down in front of Hill's Angels and wishing to be part of it.

In fairness, the Angels initially had their own spots, but Hill and Kirkland found that as soon as the Americans got hold of the shows, they re-edited them. This was done not out of any feelings of prudery or censorship but simply to cram in more advert breaks, but still. The sections that they chose to do without were the dance routines. Partly to get around this and partly to counter the growing murmurs of those spoilsport women's libbers, Hill and Kirkland broke up the dance sections and incorporated the girls into the sketches. But it was all much of the same. For all Hill's time-honoured protestations that in his sketches the male characters were always weak and the women were the strong ones, it wasn't really that way. Any flash of knicker or runaway cleavage, any exposed stocking or overspill bra, was accompanied by a camera pan to Benny and that sideways leer to the camera. That is what proved to be the undoing of him. What he never realized was that the women's libbers weren't objecting to the flesh so much as his reaction to it.

Chapter 17 Tossed Salad and Scrambled Eggs

MANY of the Hill's Angels went into the show hoping to use it as a leg up . . . sorry, hoped to use it to further their careers. To get noticed. But it rarely worked out that way. In the same way that women take jobs as secretaries hoping to get an 'in' but then find themselves typecast in their roles and not taken seriously as anything else. The Hill's Angels crew either got out of the business altogether (like Sue Upton) or did something related (like Yvonne Paul, who after she left the troupe set up her own model agency). The notable exception to this was Jane Leeves, who went from bra and suspenders to joining the cast of possibly the most successful American comedy show of the 1990s. Mind you, she had to run away to Hollywood and adopt an extraordinarily dodgy Mancunian accent to get the job as Daphne Moon in *Frasier*.

Born in 1962 in London and raised in East Grinstead, Sussex, the daughter of an engineer and a nurse, Jane modelled and was a dancer in various British shows, including *The Benny Hill Show* and *Morecambe and Wise Show* until a knee injury in 1981 forced her to stop. After that she went for more straightforward acting, but the biggest part she got was in *Monty Python's The Meaning of Life* in 1983. Again, it was a role that took advantage of the attributes that first attracted British comics.

Later that same year, Jane gave up England and headed off to try her luck in America. 'I let my apartment in London go and sold everything. I literally had $1,000

Jane Leeves seeing Dr Benny Hill before meeting Dr Frasier Crane

and a suitcase when I got on the plane. The next day I enrolled in my first acting class. We had some great people, Jim Carrey, Ellen DeGeneres, Molly Ringwald. It was very inspirational.' Despite a role in the William Friedkin thriller *To Live and Die in L.A.* in 1985, it wasn't easy. 'I was a professional babysitter and did the whole struggling actor thing. It was horrible for two years but I met some wonderful people who became great friends.' A few bits and pieces were picked up – including a controversial episode of *Seinfeld* in 1992 – before The Big Break in 1993 when she was cast as Daphne Moon in the *Cheers* spin-off, *Frasier*. 'I had heard that the casting agent for *Frasier* had said to my agent: "Don't make a move without telling me." We called the *Frasier* producers and they faxed me a scene. I read it and it was brilliantly written. I went in and read for them. Kelsey Grammer came in and read with me. We had a great chemistry and they said: "Hired."' Since then, Jane hasn't looked back. The show was an immediate hit in

At least Frasier let Daphne wear more clothes when serving dinner . . .

America (to date it has picked up sixteen Emmys) and audiences warmed to sweet, eccentric Daphne.

In the second season of *Frasier* she picked up the Viewers For Quality Television Award for Best Supporting Actress in a Comedy and last year was nominated for Best Supporting Actress in the Emmys. Everywhere it has played, *Frasier* has picked up credits and plaudits, but when it was first aired in the UK people were quick to mock that obviously fake Mancunian accent. John Mahoney, who plays Frasier's father Martin, said, 'When they cast Jane in the role of Daphne, they had no idea what someone from Manchester sounded like. Jane has more of, what I'd call a posh accent.' Jane is more pragmatic. 'Basically, this show wasn't made for an English market. The accent I use has to be understood by an American audience.'

It's a curious thing that despite her fame in America, where she does all the regular star stuff, gets mobbed in supermarkets and hangs out with the Clintons, Jane is still relatively unknown in her native England. But while not a US citizen ('I get to pay taxes, though') she considers herself an American because it was in LA that 'I became who I am'. She might be living the great American dream, but it doesn't stop her feeling hurt that she isn't well-known in Britain, and it doesn't take long for the usual points to be made. 'In Britain, people are quick to criticize success, whereas in Hollywood there's a sense that nothing is impossible. I had a dream that I wanted to be an actress and here I am, sitting in my offices on the Paramount lot, running my own company, on a hugely successful TV show with offers to do all kinds of things. Who would have thought that was possible? I drive home every day and see the Hollywood sign ahead of me, and I'm thrilled. But I never forget where I came from. I never forget what it took to get here.' And what did it take? 'Hard work, determination, and a lot of luck.'

Now that she's a big star – a very big star with a salary of £22,000 an episode and starry LA lifestyle, complete with a husband who's an executive at Paramount studios (the company that makes *Frasier*) – Jane is fairly disparaging about her humble beginnings. Ask her about Hill and she says, 'All that Benny Hill stuff is out there' in a way designed to change the subject. Yet her attitude is typical of the double standards that people use and the sense of near-embarrassment that surrounds *The Benny Hill Show*. Last year Jane publicized her new feature film by posing, yes, in bra and suspenders for *FHM* magazine. And yes, the poses were much more raunchy, more 'soft-porn' – come here boys, look at me – in attitude than anything Hill ever put out. Jane also has her own production company called – and this is even more Hillesque – Bristol Cities Productions. Bristol Cities? Rhyming slang for . . . oh, think about it. The production company, she says, is not a 'vanity project' but is there to 'find great material for myself, and try to get the English people to respect me'. Of course.

Although she's succeeded in a way that others only dream of, she is dogged by the conviction that she doesn't deserve it. 'There's a lot of that "I'm not worthy" stuff. A lot of that "I don't belong here" business. That someone's going to come along and say: "Please pack up your things and go."' Most actors suffer occasional crises of confidence, but Jane's is so bad that both her husband and sister urged her to visit a therapist when she burst into tears after seeing herself on television. 'But I won't. I'm used to living with my insecurities.'

Which takes us back to Benny Hill.

Chapter 18 Sandra and Other Stories

Interviewer: How many of your Hill's Angels have you been to bed with?
Benny Hill: Off the record, I can put my hand on my heart and tell you honestly I haven't made love to one of those girls . . . [pause] I think her name is Sandra.

THE Angels were among the few people Benny allowed to come close, and yes, of course the rumours flew. Dirty old man, beautiful young girls in a state of undress. It didn't take long for the words 'casting' and 'couch' to come into the scenario. Stefanie Marrian apart, there was no evidence for anything untoward going on at all. On the contrary, there was a story knocking about which led the casual observer to suspect nothing. It dates from the theatre days of the 1940s . . .

Benny was approached by another performer, a character called Toni, half of a novelty act called Toni and Tim. (Listen, a character called Toni. How do you think this story's going to end up?) Anyway, Toni approached Benny and said that he was looking for a new partner, why didn't they meet up and talk about it. So Benny went round to Toni's flat in Maida Vale in north London. 'Toni had a luxurious flat. Thick carpets and modern art everywhere. When I arrived, he gave me some delicious shortcake he had cooked himself, and cold lemonade. Only about five parts gin, that's all.' Then Benny did his impersonations. After one, Toni said 'You're a knockout. That Eddie Cantor

was marvellous.' Benny told him it was Al Jolson. What happened next . . . 'Come here, sit down, take the weight off your feet. Toni started talking about stardom and how much they could earn – 'another lemonade?' – when . . . 'All of a sudden he's got his hand inside my shirt, touching my chest. "Give us a kiss" he says. "What are you talking about?" "Well, if we're going to work together, we've got to be friends." "That's silly. I don't kiss men. That'd be silly."' It stayed with Benny. 'Now I realized how some ladies feel when I come on strong with "My God, you're beautiful."'

Meanwhile, back in the real world, Benny was in a double bind with the Hill's Angels. What was he? A dirty old man shagging them on the sofa as he checked their credentials? Or a poof? If it wasn't one thing, they were going to get him with another.

Sorry, what was that? Who's Stefanie Marrian? I thought you'd never ask. Stefanie Marrian was a one-time Hill's Angel who, in 1985, did that time-honoured thing. She went to the *News of the World*. I WAS BENNY HILL'S LOVE SLAVE! she announced as she told the timeless tale of the casting couch, the actress, and the wheezing old geezer who, how shall we say, needed a helping hand now and then. The way she told it, she wasn't the first and she wasn't the last. It's a fantastically *News of the World*-type story. Who knows the truth and, frankly, what does it matter? Don't you think the lawyers are rich enough already? All he said was, 'It's so unfair. She's been allowed to tell it her way, but I haven't been able to give my side. It wasn't the way she made it sound at all.'

Whatever, it's much more likely that the Angels were used by Benny not as any 'masturbatory prop' but simply as a link to the real world. Benny sat there in his little flat watching his banks of televisions, paranoid and hiding from the world, and when it all got too much or when he felt the need, he'd phone one of the Angels.

Of all the Hill's Angels, no one was closer to Hill than Sue Upton. For seventeen years they worked together, building up a relationship, a bond, that few others ever did. It was a relationship that went beyond the usual showbiz surface glitz, so much so that Sue believed that had she not already been married, Benny would have asked her.

'I knew he hardly ever went to anyone's home. He wouldn't see a soul for days on end. Then he would phone me and say, "I've still got me jimjams on. I haven't been outside for two days." And then he would talk non-stop for hours,' she said.

Sue first met Benny when she was twenty and her agent sent him her photo. This wasn't an uncommon tactic for agents looking after bubbly blondes, and the choice of girls was Benny's and only Benny's. Still, rarely did Hill see what he called 'that special twinkle' and return the call. 'When I was twenty, in April 1977, I was sent to see Benny at his flat in Queensgate, west London. We got on so well and I felt so at ease with him that I ended up spending the day with him. We had lunch and he told lots of funny jokes. Two weeks later, my agent told me that Benny had booked me for his show.'

Sue was . . . I was going to say 'vulnerable', but maybe that's the wrong choice of word. Sue was needy. 'My father died when I was three. If someone wants to step into that place, you jump at the chance.' Benny as a father substitute? Maybe. He'd probably have made a good father, able to relate to children on their terms and on their level. Benny as a father-substitute to a grown blonde model with a penchant for taking her clothes off? That I don't know. 'He was there to help and protect me. He never took advantage. He called me little Sue, little sausage or little heart. I felt safe with him.'

But it's funny. Little Sausage might feel safe with Uncle Ben, but not so safe that she felt able to share the biggest day of her life with him. When she started working on the Hill show she was engaged, but when she got married a year later, Benny didn't know. You'd have thought that maybe since she saw him as her father-replacement figure she might, at best, want him to give her away, or at least to be there. Instead, Sue kept her marriage a secret and never wore her wedding ring. 'I thought he might be hurt and not want me on the show. But when someone told him I was married he was fine. Our relationship improved. It suited him that I wasn't free. He was safe with me. I wasn't going to be lusting after him.'

Sue recalls: 'He would come to stay with us a week at a time, but even though I always invited him he would never come for Christmas. He liked to be alone then. When he stayed he treated me like a substitute wife and he'd say, "Come on Mummy, let's take the littlies out." That's what he'd call the children.' Sue's husband Roger said, 'I felt Benny treated Sue more like a daughter than a girlfriend, and he acted like a granddad to the children. He was a good mate of mine as well.'

Whatever the truth of what Stefanie said, there's no doubt that Hill felt a genuine affection for his Angels. Yvonne Paul, one of the first Angels, said, 'He had a heart of gold. He was a dear, dear friend who I knew for more than twenty years.' When her days as an Angel came to an end, Benny gave her money to set up a model agency. 'I had a very soft spot for him and I know he had one for me. The way I'll always remember him is as Uncle Benny. That's how he signed his cards to me and my daughter.' Louise English, another Angel, said, 'He was a genius and my best friend. I'll miss him more than words can ever say.'

'I was so fortunate to have worked for such a lovely, kind, generous man, and if I could turn the clock back and start all over again, I would,' said Sue. 'There are different ways of loving people and I didn't love him like a husband. He was strange, really. But then he was a comic genius and they usually are. He was selfish and childlike. He liked the closeness I gave him, but he liked to walk away from it too. He always looked at me with wonderful warmth in his face. I'll never forget him.'

Hill was still pulling in the ratings and was still being fêted outside of England, but – and these things are always easy to say in retrospect – the writing was on the wall. Part of the problem was Hill himself. He was now nearly 60, and the sight of a 60-year-old geezer running around a bunch of twentysomething semi-clads . . . it wasn't only lacking in credibility and dignity, it was starting to look disturbingly dirty. In 1983 there was a sketch where he dressed as a schoolboy and sneaked into a strip club. Cue leering looks and very skimpy stripper-type clothes. Again, it's easy to look back and comment, but you can't help but feel that Benny was playing with fire. With a sketch like that, was he baiting those feminists who'd been banging on about his show? Was he just flexing his muscles, showing that he was more powerful than they were? Was he drunk with success, the effect of so many years at the top that he felt fireproof? I'm Benny Hill. I can do what I like. Or was it that he simply didn't know what else to do?

Chapter 19 Where Next?

BY the mid-1980s the shows had become routine and formulaic. No show was complete without the sirry irriot Chow Mein. Hang about a minute. There's Fred Scuttle. Whoops! There's someone's bottom. It's impossible to stay at the top for so many years – what was it? Nearly twenty years at the top of the telly tree? – without resorting to routine and formula. Everyone in the entertainment game had their routines, their fall-back positions. The Who's guitarist Pete Townshend once said that whenever he saw his crowd getting restless or looking bored, he'd jump in the air and throw in a few windmill twirls on his guitar. It was what he did, what the crowd had come to see him do. It was what he'd worked all those years for. Similarly, John McEnroe. All those tantrums and arguments. Maybe at the start of his career he'd meant it, but by the end all he was doing was performing, playing to the crowd. What was a McEnroe match without an eruption? If there wasn't one . . . you'd want a refund. And so it was with Hill. If you sat down to watch *The Benny Hill Show* and you didn't see a handful of scantily-clad lovelies prancing around to that familiar music . . . it wouldn't be *The Benny Hill Show*. You'd want your money back. All the comedy greats fell into the same trap. Morecambe and Wise had their routines, their formulas. 'Here is a play what I wrote.' Tommy Cooper. 'Uh-huh, huh, huh.' Dick Emery. 'Oooh you are awful. But I like you.'

If anything, Hill had fallen victim to his own success and, understandably enough, was loath to change that winning formula. A 1980 sketch taking the rise out of *Butch Cassidy and the Sundance Kid*? Doesn't matter that the film was ten years old. It gave Hill (Butch) a chance to slap Wright (the Kid) around. However limp the set-up, however predictable the outcome, it gave everyone a chance to do what they did, a chance to play their solos.

Looking back at it, Hill's longevity is a bit of a marvel. Not long ago we were saying that 1971 proved a bit of a high water mark for Hill. Well, 1980 was another high water mark. The Americans were totally infatuated with him, couldn't get enough. British critics were starting to reappraise his work, figuring that if the Americans loved him then maybe there was something going on that they were missing. Thames, it doesn't need to be said, were in love with him. But then again, back in 1980, Thames had it all wrapped up. Tommy Cooper, Morecambe and Wise, Benny Hill. They had them all.

Maybe it was Hill's success in America that was decisive in sorting out his choice of material. Aware that it was the saucy slapstick stuff that appealed, he concentrated more and more on that sort of material. The clever wordplays and sketches that played with British culture and British television mores took a backseat to the more Mack Sennett inspired chases.

Chapter 20 The Last Benny Hill Sketch

'In the late Eighties, Benny was getting a tremendous amount of stick about the sexism thing which was giving him grief. To console himself, he was obviously drinking more than I remembered him drinking in the Seventies. One day he came into work and he was desperately upset. "I saw Billy Connolly on the box last night and he said the F word eighteen times," Benny said, appalled. "No one bats an eyelid, but I get slaughtered for appreciating the female form. The gag on my show is always that the men are being trodden on by the women. Why can't they see that?" About a year later, Benny was sacked and he was devastated. I'm sure all the strain and the comfort drinking contributed to his heart attack in 1992. After his second heart attack he called me from the hospital. "Little Heart, I'm fit and raring to go," he said. He knew I had a fitness video coming out and said, "Let's get together and do some workout photos. Let's show the world I'm not beaten yet." Two weeks later he was dead.'

Libby Roberts, dancer 1972–5, choreographer 1982–9

BENNY Hill was killed by Ben Elton. It's not really true, but for a while it was a great story. Benny v Benny. Old v New. Establishment v radical. Fat sexist pig v enlightened committed liberal. It's a great story.

In 1986, Ben Elton gave an interview in which he said that he could find nothing funny in Benny Hill's little old man chasing girls round the park when the incidence of rape was up and it was unsafe for women to be in parks at night. And that was that. From that moment on, Benny Hill was history. It didn't matter that his show was still showing in over 100 countries. Didn't matter that he was probably still 'the world's most famous comedian'. It was curtains. Listen, when the *Sun* runs a leader about your sexism, it's time to get out.

In April 1989, John Howard Davies, the new head of Light Entertainment, called Benny Hill into his office. Ten minutes later Benny and Dennis Kirkland were sitting in their favourite pub. A stunned silence passed between the two men as they wondered how it was they'd just been sacked.

If Benny's 1970s output can partially be explained (if maybe not justified) by placing it in its cultural context, his fall from grace in the Britain of the 1980s can also be explained by the same methods. In the late 1970s we'd had the punk revolution, something that might seem irrelevant to The Benny Hill Story, but that actually was pivotal. Punk wasn't just about the Sex Pistols and the Clash, punk really was anarchy in the UK. It turned everything upside down, destroyed all the old certainties and pulled the rug from under the feet of just about everyone. It was as much a cultural watershed as the war had been. Life before punk and life after punk are two completely distinct and separate beasts. Punk stuck a rocket up everyone's fundament, not just the old Establishment (in the case of our story, the Hills of the world) but also the angry brigade (again, in our story, the feminist lobby). Before punk, the feminist lobby was all middle-class theory and banners. But . . . that was never going to cut any ice once Gaye Advert was standing on stage.

That old punk ethic – anyone can do it – gave comedy a whole new impetus. Once places like The Comedy Store sprang up people like Benny Hill were always going to be vulnerable. Young comics were circling, eager for a piece of the action. Programmes like *The Young Ones* were soon cutting a swathe through the schedules. OK, so it was on BBC2, but it was the shape of things to come. When Tommy Cooper, Eric Morecambe and Leonard Rossiter all died in quick succession it was like someone celestial was making space for the new arrivals.

It wasn't that there wasn't room for both the Rik Mayalls and the Benny Hills, it was just that, when compared with the new breed, Hill looked so old-fashioned. Adrian Edmondson would come in, head-butt the fridge and kick through a door.

Benny Hill would come and do Fred Scuttle. Again. I'm not sure that Scuttle ever had anything to say, but now he looked just like he was supposed to look, like an idiot. Hill was like a wounded animal. The years of criticism had, despite his huge ratings, made him weak. Maybe it was those huge ratings that undermined him. He was undoubtedly complacent by then, resting on his laurels. It might have been pulling in the punters, but it had been a long time since Benny Hill had been surprising, let alone cutting-edge.

It's an irony that, to Hill aficionados, his later shows decline precisely because he'd listened to the women's libbers and had toned down his ideas. In 1987, Hill called Libby Roberts, his choreographer. 'One day I got a call from him and he said, "Dear Heart, I want you to choreograph the Hill's Angels and clean up the act a bit." He was very aware of public opinion. So we did more operatic things, like throwing in a bit of *Carmen*, and toning down the raunchiness.'

Have you ever seen a huge ocean tanker, loaded with oil, try to turn round? OK, it's unlikely. What are you? The sort of person who hangs around in the middle of an ocean? But you know the story. With all that momentum, they take miles and miles to make any sort of turn. It's a slow and painful procedure. Well, Benny Hill was that huge ocean tanker, and in truth the change of course didn't improve things. That the girls wore a few more clothes didn't stop them being sex objects. They were still there. That they fought back and took even less crap from the men in the scripts didn't make any difference either. That just fuelled other S&M fantasies. Hill's way of dealing with the criticism was like much of what he did. There was no bad intent, no malice. It was just another illustration of his total lack of understanding, his utterly childlike sexual naïvety. Listen, you get criticism because you're objectifying women, treating them as objects. So what do you do? You dress them up in sexy cowboy outfits and you get them to – literally – walk all over the men. It's bizarre. He's either absolutely on the button and taking the piss in the extreme, or he simply doesn't get it.

Still more confusingly, Hill's Angels were replaced by Hill's Little Angels. What was that about? It's beyond any sort of logic. Forget the shows for a minute. This is a man whose life is coming under an increasingly heavy scrutiny by an increasingly intrusive and censorious press. All sorts of scurrilous rumours are flying about. There's talk of trips to Thailand, to the Philippines, to these faraway places where, for a price, you can get anything you desire. The rumours, not to put too fine a point on it, were – how shall we say? – age-based. At which point Benny Hill replaces the Hill's Angels (grown-ups) with Hill's Little Angels (children). It's beyond any sort of logic.

In 1989 John Howard Davies made a speech at Montreux and talked of change in the air. It's what happens when a new person takes over: they always talk of change and doing things their way. But Benny Hill didn't worry. Why should he worry? He was still the biggest star in the sky, still the jewel in the crown. And he was still fêted abroad. In April 1989, Benny and Dennis were received like visiting royalty in Cannes. OK, so the French sometimes have a different take on matters of comedy from the rest of the world (look at the case of Jerry Lewis), but his shows were still being shown there and were still pulling in huge audiences. He was making buckets of cash for Thames. What did he have to fear?

'I don't want to do any more Bennys,' said John Howard Davies. Well, that's quite straightforward, isn't it? His decision was attacked by Hillites as barbaric, and even now it's seen as cruel and heartless. Poor old Benny. Never did nothing to no one.

Howard Davies won't talk about it now – apparently he feels he's been scapegoated – but although his decision was harsh, you can see why he took it. Compared to everything else that Thames was producing, Hill's shows cost a fortune. While he was pulling in 20 million-odd viewers, that was acceptable. Every station needs its big-money flagship. But by 1988 the figure had fallen to less than half of that; it was in free-fall. The accountants were getting twitchy. The advertisers didn't want to be associated with the programme any more, and for them more than anyone, the figures told the story.

Television is a hard-nosed, commercial enterprise. That's the beginning and the end of it, and if Hill had still been doing the business, pulling in the punters, you can bet your life that Howard Davies would have toughed out the storm and waited for the Benny Hill backlash to subside, as it most certainly would have. But Hill wasn't doing the business. Even his greatest admirers would have to admit that he wasn't as good as he had been – over the hill, you might say. He was less sharp, less inventive, less imaginative – he simply wasn't as funny as he had been – and there was no sign that it would change. After all, there was a new, more street-smart crowd on the rise. If Howard Davies had kept faith with Hill and the downward trend had continued . . . that would have been Davies's career down the pan. Rather than hang on in with a knackered pony, Howard Davies decided to get out while he could and go for something new. That his something new was *Mr Bean*, well, it can only have added insult to injury.

Benny was like a deer gone lame. Helpless. It didn't take long for the hyenas to come sniffing around and the vultures to start circling. Former Hill's Angels came out of the woodwork telling of Benny's curious working methods and strange hobbies. Others told of how he would invite them round for drinks and nibbles. They told their stories, and maybe when they'd finished telling their tale they'd go to the bank with their paying-in book. All that tabloid tat, it's not nice but it's the nature of the fame game. One of the aspects of this story that make it really sad is that Benny never played the fame game. He didn't get the benefits. He just got the crap. But that, I guess, was his fault. He was, after all, a funny geezer. Other stories started coming out, some disturbing, some comical. He took dodgy holidays. He used carrier bags. Stories. They were all worth a cheque.

It was the usual sordid stuff, but it helped install a picture of Benny in the public's eye that was more and more unsavoury. Increasingly fat, increasingly sweaty, red-faced and disturbingly childlike. It didn't help that his face didn't really age. He didn't get lines. He didn't go bald. He just kept looking like a strange man-boy, somehow retarded, trapped in a world that was totally alien to him and increasingly unfriendly.

Later, Hill said, 'It would be nice to have a TV show here, but it was a blessing in disguise when mine was dropped. One gets complacent after forty years.' He should worry, though. Compared with the way the television industry treated Ernie Wise, he got away lightly.

CHAPTER 21 Central Perk

AS 1991 turned into 1992, it looked as though things might be on the up for Benny Hill. It had been three years since that heart-breaking sacking – more than long enough for a man to sit in the ante-room waiting for his time to come again. Frankie Howerd had been exhumed. Why not Benny? Just as importantly, all those angry young pups who'd been so quick to criticize Hill on their way up the ladder were now part of the comedy Establishment themselves. It's the way of life. The new pretenders always criticize the established kings, because they know who holds the crown, and they want it. Criticizing is simply a sophisticated, refined way of throwing down the gauntlet. Looked at in a certain light, that's all that happened to Hill. When the challenge has been made and the old king has been defeated, the challenger simply takes his place. It's rare that very much changes in terms of form or structure. It's only ever the face. Thus it was in 1992 when it came to casting *Carry On Columbus*. Faced with the troublesome fact that most of the original *Carry On* crew were dead, the producers had little problem filling their shoes. They picked up their cell-phones and called . . . and the massed ranks of the 'alternative comedy' scene came running.

But two things were to stop Benny hitting the heights again. First, he died – not that there aren't plenty of dead rock stars and actors who'd tell you if they could that it was the best career move they ever made. The main thing that stopped Benny Hill being welcomed back into the fold was that he never recognized how much the world had changed, or if he did, he didn't build that change into his humour. When he was rehabilitated, Frankie Howerd adapted and turned himself into a post-ironic version of himself, though in fairness maybe he always had been. But when Benny Hill was given a chance to get back into the arena, he didn't embrace the new, he simply went back to where he'd stood before.

Shortly before his death in 1992, Hill started work on his first television show for three years. *Benny Hill's World Tour* was conceived as three one-hour specials, each one filmed and conceived for a specific region in the world where Benny was particularly popular. Australia and the Far East were pencilled in, but the kick-off was in New York. Though it was Taffner's idea to film the show there, Hill soon got into it. 'I want the subject of our sketches to be part of US culture,' he said. But viewed now, the material doesn't seem to have taken on board any of the criticisms that led him to be sacked from Thames, the same criticisms that seemed to have hit him so hard.

While it's natural to surround yourself with the familiar after such a long break – and maybe it was the equivalent of the comfort eating (and drinking) that Hill was so familiar with – you do tend to wonder what he was thinking of when he included yet another gratuitous shot of Sue Upton's bottom in a sketch about a bank robbery. There were other comfort zones. A sketch where the gags revolved around Bob Todd's linguistically incompetent German: Hill finds himself in hospital and instead of the normal dolly birds you find in a hospital (if you're Benny Hill), he gets lumbered with Bob Todd in drag. Jokes from Plotsk are dusted off and given artificial resuscitation ('I make love almost every night. Almost on Monday. Almost on Tuesday . . .'). Mr Chow Mein came on and did his turn. In a sense it's fair enough. The Americans loved all this stuff, and the show was aimed at and made for that American market, so in a sense Hill was just pleasing his public. That's what they want to see. It makes them happy. So why not? There was a feeling of militant nostalgia – Why not replay the old gags? Why not wheel out the old faithfuls? On the other hand . . . there was a definite sense of safety in familiarity.

In a final act of defiance/lack of imagination, the show ended with Benny pursued by young women. OK, so it was in Central Park, but the real location was locked inside Hill's head. It was such a blatant gesture, it makes you wonder whether he'd done it as a riposte to those English critics who'd directed their venom towards him: 'Look, you lot might reckon I'm washed up and that this brand of humour is past its sell-by date, but the Americans still love it, they still love me.' It would be nice to think that that was Hill's motivation – it would credit him with fighting spirit – but there's precious little evidence to suggest that he had that much fight left in him.

When the show was finally aired in Britain in 1994, executive producer Don Taffner said that Hill had been suffering from melancholy, and was still depressed at the way he'd been treated. 'Benny was very happy during the filming but terribly melancholy as soon as it finished. He felt really hurt the way he was treated in the UK.'

Chapter 22 The Final Act

BENNY Hill died on Saturday, 18 April 1992. He was 68. He'd been ill for some time, overweight and depressed, he'd taken to drink and comfort-eating, which had both combined to make him even more overweight and depressed. It's the way.

After his contract was cancelled, Benny had nowhere to go. Nowhere spiritually, nowhere physically, nowhere emotionally. It was a difficult time. He couldn't take refuge in his family, because he had none. He couldn't do a spot of shopping therapy, because it wasn't in his nature. He never had before and it was too late to shop now. So he drank and he ate. And he got overweight and depressed.

Things had been starting to look up. At the beginning of 1992, Central TV had been playing with the idea of bringing back Ben. Philip Jones had brokered a deal and talks had been talked. Central had been less than impressed by the American show but Benny's people persuaded them that their man wasn't really washed up, he'd just tailored his show for the specific market. A deal was done. Confidence was high (well, high-ish) so Hill and Kirkland sat down to write.

But it was now that all the overweight and depressed business came back to haunt him. On 9 February 1992, he was due at Central but . . . What are those chest pains? A mild heart attack is a body shouting out for help and that's what Benny's was doing. He was taken to hospital and, once safely wrapped up in their cotton wool, he relaxed -- and had a proper heart attack. That was on 11 February. A bypass operation was suggested, but Benny refused. Maybe he knew what the story was, maybe he knew that it was time. Whatever, he said that he wanted things to heal naturally, he wanted his heart to mend itself. But a broken heart doesn't mend that easily. After eight days he was released. Standing on the steps of the hospital, rent-a-nurse in hand, Ben stoically did his stupid Scuttle salute and went home.

But he was only home for two weeks before . . . he was back. Another heart attack. This time it was serious. He was told to lose at least two stone, but how much ache can one heart take? Curiously, one of his visitors in hospital was Michael Jackson. Wacko Jacko, another social curio who, it might come as no great surprise to learn, was a great fan of Benny's. It's a funny thing. Michael Jackson and Charlie Chaplin were two of Benny's biggest showbiz fans. Jacko came to visit and before the day was out the two had hatched a plan for Benny to appear in Jackson's new video. It's a shame it came to nothing. It would have been funny. Benny dancing in a Michael Jackson video. But while back at home in his mum's house in Southampton, before Benny could moonwalk to Neverland, he died.

No one really knows what happened that Saturday night in April 1992. Not the neighbours who noticed that the light was on but couldn't hear the tell-tale sound of the omnipresent television. Not the police who the neighbours called. Not Dennis Kirkland who the police called. But that's what happens when you die alone. It was very sad, but no great surprise. He was a very ill man. Hill's body was found, naturally enough, by the ever-faithful Dennis Kirkland. It seemed only right.

Two days later, Thames put out an appreciation programme called, appropriately, *Benny Hill – An Appreciation*. For Thames, this was an awkward time. Here was the company that dumped Hill, the company that dropped him in the middle of Desolation Row. And now they had to eulogize, to stand and give all the usual obituary platitudes. To John Howard Davies's credit, he never did. A parade of comics from Hill's generation spoke of the great man and, making reference to the sad fact that Frankie Howerd died a day later on 19 April, cracked gags about being number three. It was Woody Allen who said that 'comedy = tragedy + time' and though this application of the equation doesn't include much time, there was an extra ingredient in it: comedy = tragedy + time + fear.

The aftermath of Benny Hill's death was as confused as his life. There he was, dead, with an estimated £10 million fortune sitting waiting to be collected. But there was no obvious next of kin. When the police had to call someone they called Kirkland, but that wasn't the answer.

Hill had earned buckets, but had never learned how to spend it. He gave money to charity, he gave money to good causes. He left cheques uncashed while cash went unchecked. There was a big cake left. Various interested parties staked a claim, but the truth was that the last time Hill had made a will it was in 1961 when he left everything to his parents, and they were long gone. Sue Upton, the Hilliest of the Angels, said: 'Benny had no idea what money meant to people because it meant nothing to him. He did tell me that I was in his will. "Don't worry, little sausage," he used to say; "when I'm gone, you and the littlies won't have any money worries." His death came as a double blow. First, because Central TV was about to revive his career and I was about to sign a lucrative contract to appear in two more shows. Second, because no one ever found a new will. There was only an old one which had left everything to his parents, and they'd been dead a long time. Imagine how it was: one minute I felt like I'd won the Lottery because Benny was worth millions and the next minute there was nothing.' What type of person writes a will and leaves everything to their parents? In the normal scheme of things, who expects their parents to outlive them?

The tabloid spotlight fell on two unlikely faces. There were two disabled women – Jeanette Warner and Phoebe King ('Netta' and 'Kitten') – who Hill had befriended. These women had been like sisters to Hill and were as close as anyone ever got. That's not a lot, you understand, but it was something. Warner had died a few months before Hill in February, but King was still alive. Kitten didn't know how to play the game – why should she? How many famous people know how to deflect the lizards? What chance did a little old lady stand? After the usual undignified media feeding frenzy, King was identified, variously, as Hill's lover, Hill's sister, Hill's fiancée, Hill's muse, Hill's pet cat. In the end, of course, she was none of the above. She was just a little old lady who a sad lonely old man had befriended.

Because the beneficiaries of the will were both dead, the estate went to his brother Leonard and his sister Diana, neither of whom he'd enjoyed the closest of relationships with. But there was a problem there, too. Leonard and Diana were also dead. But between them they had seven children and so the estate – the money, an estimated £7 million – went to them. A note was found among Benny's effects listing names (Upton, English, Kirkland) with sums of money – but then what's an unsigned, unwitnessed piece of paper worth?

The funeral was held on 28 April and, in its way, it was a fitting end. No stars, no showbiz pals, just his 'family' (McGee, Upton, Kirkland, *et al*) and the people of Southampton. It was probably the way he'd have wanted it, just as it was when they laid his body to rest, in a grave next to his mum and dad, the headstone engraved with the word 'Reunited'.

Benny and Bob Todd cracking jokes outside the pearly gates

Epilogue

'His funeral was as cryptic as his life had been. The fact that he was a world-famous comedian was made obvious by the streets of Southampton lined with weeping faces. But there was only a smattering of people at the actual funeral, and very few from the world of showbiz. As a tribute to Benny, the women attending had all agreed to wear suspenders underneath their skirts. So we all sat there in the pews with stockings and suspenders hidden, and when the service ended they played the famous Benny Hill theme tune. It was comic and tragic at the same time, which summed up dear old Benny.'

Yvonne Paul, one of Benny's dancers, 1970–1